♠ ♣ ♥ ♦

Texas Hold'em Odds and Probabilities

Limit, No-Limit, and Tournament Strategies

♠ ♣ ♥ ♦

First Edition

By
Matthew Hilger

Dimat Enterprises, Inc.
www.InternetTexasHoldem.com

Texas Hold'em Odds and Probabilities: Limit, No-Limit, and Tournament Strategies.
Copyright © 2006 by Matthew Hilger.
Published by Dimat Enterprises, Inc.

Cover Illustration and CD Layout: Angela Adams
Book Design: Andrew and Eva Kuczynski

ISBN 0-9741502-2-3

Matthew Hilger is also author of *Internet Texas Hold'em*, published by Dimat Enterprises, Inc.

About Dimat Enterprises, Inc. and Dimat Online, Inc.

Dimat Enterprises, Inc. is a publishing company founded by Matthew Hilger. Matthew also started Dimat Online, Inc. which operates Matthew's website, www.InternetTexasHoldem.com. The two companies offer online and print media within the poker industry.

Books

Internet Texas Hold'em, by Matthew Hilger, published in 2003.

Texas Hold'em Odds and Probabilities: Limit, No-Limit, and Tournament Strategies, by Matthew Hilger, published in 2006.

The Poker Mindset, by Ian Taylor and Matthew Hilger, is planned for the fall of 2006.

Matthew and his wife Diana donate $1 for every book sold to Colombianitos, a charity founded in Atlanta, Georgia that helps children in need in Colombia. For more details on Colombianitos, visit www.colombianitos.org.

Website, www.InternetTexasHoldem.com
"The best poker community on the web, period."

www.InternetTexasHoldem.com, commonly known as ITH, is operated by Dimat Online, Inc. and is one of the most popular poker content sites in the world. ITH receives thousands of daily visitors and is regarded as one of the best sites on the web to help improve your game. ITH contains a wide variety of information and resources including:

♠ **The Poker Tutor** – See the cards, thoughts, and actions of professional poker players in an online setting while they demonstrate correct play. This application is one of the best teaching tools in the market. Contributors include Matthew as well as members of The Hendon Mob, consisting of Joe Beevers, Barny and Ross Boatman, and Ram Vaswani. The CD in this book gives you access to all of the "test your skills" hands from the book using The Poker Tutor application.

♦ **Internet Player of the Year** – The first objective ranking system of Internet players based on money finishes in all of the major online tournaments

♠ **Forum** – A free poker discussion group with thousands of members discussing poker strategy, bonuses, and current events within the poker world

♣ **Poker Bonuses** – A listing of the best online poker bonuses

♥ **Poker Leagues** – The Poker Leagues give players a chance to develop their skills and win great prizes, including a seat to the WSOP main event

♦ **Poker Odds Calculator** – Visitors may calculate odds for every type of Hold'em situation including scenarios against random hands or against a range of hands

♠ **Articles and Online News** – Unique articles written by some of the top online players in the World

About the Author

Matthew Hilger lives in Atlanta, Georgia with his wife, Diana, and two sons, Joshua and Zachary. Matthew received his Bachelor's degree in Finance from the University of Georgia in 1989. He completed a Master's degree in Finance at Georgia State University in 1991 as well as a Master's degree in International Business from Thunderbird in 1996.

Prior to embarking on a poker career, Matthew worked in various accounting, finance, and consulting positions with Andersen Consulting (currently Accenture), Chiquita Brands International, and Bristol-Myers Squibb. His studies and work gave Matthew the opportunity to live in Mexico, Venezuela, Costa Rica, Argentina, and New Zealand.

Matthew started playing professionally on the Internet in 2001 and has logged thousands of hours online, playing at limits from $1-$2 up to $100-$200 and in countless online tournaments. Matthew's first book, *Internet Texas Hold'em* was released in August 2003 and became one of the top-selling poker books in the world.

Matthew's tournament accomplishments include winning the 2002 New Zealand Poker Championship and finishing 33rd out of 2576 entrants in the 2004 World Series Main Event. In the 2005 WSOP, Matthew cashed a total of three times while also making the money for the 2nd year in a row in the main event.

Matthew now devotes a lot of his working time to his website and poker forum, www.InternetTexasHoldem.com, where he answers questions about his books and general poker strategy.

Matthew's other interests, outside of poker, include composing on the piano and traveling. His travels have taken him to over 25 countries throughout Europe, Latin America, the Caribbean, and "down under."

Dedication

To my family, Diana, Joshua, and Zachary who supported me all the times I was away working on this book.

Acknowledgements

This book could not have been completed without the help, advice, and suggestions from so many people. When I embarked on writing this book, I knew that I had a tremendous resource to tap to help me – the poker forum at my website. We have the best poker community on the web and the amount of volunteers that came forward to help me with this book only helped confirm this. There were so many volunteers that I had to turn some of them down.

I would first like to acknowledge everyone at the Forum for supporting me in all of my poker endeavors. Their support, advice, suggestions, and criticisms have helped me become the player and writer that I am today. I could not have finished this book without their support and help.

A big thanks goes out to Angela Adams, aka Angel-Fish, for designing the book cover and CD layout. Her design was the hands-down winner in the competition we had on the Forum for the book cover.

The following Forum members helped edit the book by providing content suggestions and overall general comments on the readability and flow:

Ammon Brown, aka Ammbo
Paul Ferner, aka PauliF
Jane Griscti, aka JaneG
Neal Nicholson, aka LuckyDog
Tony Pillinger, aka Pilchard
Matt Rousu, aka Poker_Elmo
Erik Rand, aka Ezplayer
Albert Sands, aka Sandsstorm
Terry Steer, aka Ts911993

A good poker book should have lots of hand examples to show how the concepts work in practice. The difficult part in providing hand examples is finding real examples that demonstrate a specific point I am trying to convey as an author. With that in mind, I asked members of the Forum to send in hand examples on different topics and was overwhelmed with the response. The result is that I had a great database of hands to choose from to ensure that specific topics were covered within the hand examples. The following members submitted hands that were included in the final printing:

Timothy Allen, aka TA
Kyle Barger
Florian Brezinski, aka Florian
Kevin Chan, aka Tilter
Bill Clark, aka Deacon86
Neil Dewhurst, aka Cybrarian
Jane Griscti, aka JaneG
Jason98
Christian Kjellströmm, aka Kjell201
Matt Krieg, aka Raalphd6
Dan Matthews, aka Monobrow
Don McNabb, aka McFoldem
Chris Miller, aka Cript
Michael Niedzwiecki, aka Cmjsons
James Neuman, aka Wynton
Ed Parks, aka Aupanner
Chris Platt, aka Chrisjp
Erik Rand, aka Ezplayer
Terry Steer, aka ts911933
Terry Wynn, aka Darvon

A special thanks to Troy Headrick, aka BernardDogs, for providing grammar edits and for helping the book read much smoother.

I want to also thank the Suwanee library. This became my home away from home to work on the book and I'm not sure how I would have finished if not for the cubbyhole on the southeast side!

I also want to thank the ITH team who runs our website, www.InternetTexasHoldem.com. The team at the time of printing consisted of:

Albert Sands – Chief Operating Officer
Chris Parsons – Website Administrator
Bill Limings – Customer Support
John Price – Programmer

All of these guys joined the team since I started writing the book, which gives a good indication of the growth of the site. Without their hard work I would not have been able to find the time to complete this book.

Finally, this book could not have been completed without my beautiful wife, Diana, and mother-in-law, Teresa Trujillo, keeping the house and kids in order while I was away writing. Thanks for your support, understanding, and sacrifices, especially when it looked as if I would never complete the book!

Table of Contents

Applying Odds and Probabilities in No-Limit Hold'em

Charts and Stats

Introduction

Odds and probabilities form the foundation around every single decision you will make at the poker table. Consider these examples that show how odds and probabilities impact different poker decisions:

♥ You decide to play a hand because the *probability* that you will win is high enough to justify the amount you must risk given a certain expectation on how big the pot will be. In essence, you determine that there is a positive ***expectation*** in playing the hand.

♣ The most common reason to raise is to build a larger pot with a hand that has the best *odds* to win.

♠ You might also raise to drive out opponents to improve the *odds* that your hand will win the pot.

♦ You might draw to a gut-shot straight because the *odds* of improving your hand justify a call once you have considered the size of the pot.

♥ You decide to bluff when you think there is a high enough *probability* that your opponent will fold once the bet is considered in relation to the size of the pot.

♣ You might play a weak hand now to show to your opponents to increase the *odds* of getting paid off later when you play a strong hand.

When you break it down, every single poker decision is in some way related to odds and probabilities. You do not have to be a mathematical wiz to be successful at poker. However, the more you understand the simple math behind every decision you make, the better your decisions will be. And anyone can do it...if you can add, multiply, and divide then you can calculate probabilities.

The goal of this book is to help you apply odds and probabilities to make better decisions in Texas Hold'em. We will cover all forms of the game, including limit, No-Limit, and tournament situations. Although we will walk through many of the calculations[1], the emphasis is on the application of the odds to make better strategic decisions. In addition, a comprehensive collection of Texas Hold'em charts and statistics is

---

[1] Most of the calculations in this book are straightforward. I have attempted to present the mathematical calculations in a way that most people will be able to understand logically. To do so, I avoided using combinatorial mathematics or other methods that people more advanced in math might prefer.

provided to give you the stats needed to evaluate specific situations you are likely to encounter.

While the charts and stats are important for reference, we will also look at their relevance and how they can be applied in different situations. These charts will give every serious Hold'em player one single resource to all of the important stats and probabilities they should know to help with their success as a poker player.

Understanding how often events will occur can help you effectively evaluate a given situation. Some questions this book will answer:

♥ What are the odds of your opponent holding a pocket pair when he raises first-in?
♦ What is the probability that an over-card will flop when you are holding JJ?
♠ How often does each starting hand win compared to every other hand in a heads-up battle?
♣ How often will your starting hand win against a random hand?
♥ How do you determine if drawing is profitable or not?

The applications of odds in poker go on and on. If this book does not answer one of your questions, hopefully you will now have the tools to calculate the answer for yourself.

Best of luck and I hope we meet someday in the near future at a final table!

About This Book

Those of you who have read my first book, *Internet Texas Hold'em (ITH)*, will be familiar with the organization and presentation of this book. *Texas Hold'em Odds and Probabilities* follows a similar format. Each chapter is divided into three sections similar to what you find in a textbook: text, chapter summary, and "Test Your Skills".

I received a lot of feedback about *ITH* and many readers found the chapter summaries to be quite helpful in reviewing the main concepts given in each chapter. There is quite a lot of material in this book and you will probably find yourself going back to review the book from time to time. The chapter summaries will facilitate the review process so that you can then decide where you need to go into the text for more detail.

ITH has a chapter focused on Odds and Probabilities. Some of the same concepts are presented in this book and continued readers of *ITH* will find some overlap. However, the *Applying Odds and Probabilities in Limit Hold'em* section in this book is much more detailed. The concepts in this book are broken down into beginning and advanced concepts and there are additional concepts that were not discussed in *ITH*. And, of course, the *Test Your Skills* hand examples are completely new.

Test Your Skills

The *Test Your Skills* section at the end of each chapter gives you the opportunity to practice the strategies and concepts you have learned from the text. The basic format will offer you a sequence of events that have occurred during a hand followed by a decision prompt.

The success of *Internet Texas Hold'em* was due, in large part, to the hand examples. When I first started out playing and studying Hold'em, I found that it was difficult sometimes to absorb written concepts without seeing them in action. The best poker books give a lot of hand examples for you to try and "test your skills". I give Bob Ciaffone and Jim Brier credit for encouraging the use of hand examples in their poker articles and also in their book *Middle Limit Holdem Poker*. Since the release of *Middle Limit Holdem Poker*, many new poker books now include a lot of hand examples.

If you like the examples in this book, I encourage you to read *Middle Limit Hold'em*, which has over 500 hand examples. And if you have not done so already, read *Internet Texas Hold'em*, which has over 200 hand examples. Both of those books focus on Limit Hold'em. For No-Limit, the *Harrington on Hold'em* volumes by Dan Harrington and Bill Robertie contain a good number of hand examples.

Most of the hand examples in this book were submitted from members of the discussion forum at my site, www.InternetTexasHoldem.com. With thousands of members, the forum is an excellent place to discuss poker strategy. I encourage you to check out the forum and join the discussion. If you are playing and find a situation where you are faced with a difficult decision, post in the forum and you will get plenty of feedback from other members to give you valuable perspectives.

When reading through the hand examples in this book, it is important to realize that the play of the particular player is not always correct but usually reasonable. Nevertheless, the scenario will guide you through the hand and then ask what you would do next given the sequence of events, even though you may not agree with all of the player's moves up to that point.

For each question, I give my recommended "answer" to the problem. I recommend that you answer the question first before reading my answer and explanation. To help prevent you from "cheating", I offer a short answer, raise, call, or fold, at the end of the explanation. My answers are meant to demonstrate the best strategy to use *most* of the time against *typical* opponents. The typical opponent in these examples is neither a **shark** nor a *fish* unless otherwise indicated.

Hold'em is a complex game and there are many situations that do not have clear-cut answers. For example, you could present a certain situation to 100 poker professionals and 1/3 might fold, 1/3 might call, and 1/3 might raise. Most of the questions in the book are pretty clear, but there are some that have answers that are very close. The important thing is to understand the thinking process that goes into each decision. I will usually indicate if two answers are very close and will offer an explanation for the different alternatives.

How to Calculate Odds and Probabilities

For most of us, our last math class was back in high school or, perhaps, our freshman year in college. For some of us that might not have been very long ago, but for many of us it is a distant memory! In either case, this chapter is meant to be a refresher class in some basic mathematical computations to help us look at how we will use probability calculations for different situations. The calculations we will discuss are not that difficult and can be done with any basic calculator. Those proficient in math may want to skip this chapter.

Basic Math

Fractions, Decimals, and Percentages

Fractions are one way of expressing probabilities such as "you have a one in three chance of improving." This would be written as 1/3. The numerator is the top number in the fraction or "1" in this example. The denominator is the bottom number or "3" in this example. In most of the calculations in this book you will want to convert fractions to decimals or percentages. To convert to a decimal, you simply divide 1 by 3 to get .33. To convert this decimal to a percentage, you multiply by 100 to get 33%.

For example, the probability of being dealt an ace for your first card is 4/52 (four aces in a deck of 52 cards).
- ♣ 4/52 = 1/13 = 0.077
- ♥ The percentage is 7.7% (0.077 × 100)
- ♦ In other words, you have a 1 in 13 chance of being dealt an ace on the first card, which equates to 1/13, 0.077, or 7.7% of the time.

To convert a percentage to a decimal you simply divide by 100. For example, 7.7%/100 = 0.077. Note that this is the opposite to what we did above where we multiplied a decimal by 100 to get a percentage.

To add fractions, you first need to convert the fractions to a common denominator. Once you have a common denominator you simply add the numerators together and place the result over the common denominator. For another example, add 2/4 and 3/5.

♠ First determine a common denominator. Multiply 2/4 × 5/5 to get 10/20 and multiply 3/5 × 4/4 to get 12/20.

♣ Now that you have a common denominator of 20, simply add the numerators together to get 22 (10 + 12) and place over the denominator of 20.

♦ The answer is 2/4 + 3/5 = 10/20 + 12/20 = 22/20, which is the same as 11/10.

When multiplying fractions you simply multiply the numerators together to get the new numerator and multiply the denominators together to get the new denominator. For example, 2/4 × 3/5 = (2×3) / (4×5) = 6/20 which is the same as 3/10 or 0.3.

For another example, multiply 11/50 × 10/49 × 9/48.

♣ Calculate the numerator: 11 × 10 × 9 = 990

♠ Calculate the denominator: 50 × 49 × 48 = 117,600

♦ 990/117,600 = 0.0084

♥ 0.0084 × 100 = .84% or a little less that 1%.

This calculation just determined the probability that you will flop a flush when holding two cards of the same suit…the magic of probabilities!

You will not have to do this type of complex math on a regular basis while sitting at the table. The calculations are provided here simply to give a foundation for how things are calculated. For those not interested in doing the calculations, memory can serve you just as well for common probability scenarios.

We discuss calculating probabilities in the next section but here is the detailed reasoning for the flush example. There are 52 total cards in a deck. Since we hold two cards, there are 50 cards remaining in the deck.

There are 13 cards of each suit so there are 11 of the same suit remaining in the deck. The probability that the first card on the flop will match our suit is 11/50. The probability for the second is 10/49 and for the third, 9/48. Multiplying these three probabilities together gives us the probability that all three events will occur sequentially to give us our flush.

Probabilities and Odds

Probabilities tell you how often a certain event *will* occur. They are often expressed as a fraction. For example, you have a ½ chance of getting heads when tossing a coin. This is also the same as .5 or 50%. But what if we want to know the probability of flopping heads twice in a row?

Key Concept: To calculate the probability of two or more events occurring sequentially you simply multiply the individual probabilities of each event together.

For example, ½ × ½ = ¼ or 0.25 or 25%.

What are the odds that a couple will have all boys if they want to have three kids? This is simply ½ × ½ × ½ = 1/8 or 0.125 or 12.5%.

We can apply this concept to a deck of cards with a couple more examples. What is the probability of being dealt a pocket pair?
- ♥ Your first card is a given since we are not specifying a particular pocket pair.
- ♦ Once you are dealt your first card, there are three remaining cards that will give you a pair, leaving you a 3/51 chance of matching it on the next card.
- ♣ 3/51 = 1/17 = 0.0588 or a little less than 6% of the time.

What is the probability of being dealt a pair of aces? This example requires two events to occur sequentially.
- ♥ The probability of receiving an ace for your first card is 4/52, or 1/13.

♦ After being dealt your first ace, there are three aces left within the 51 remaining cards. Therefore, you have a 3/51 chance of being dealt the second ace, or 1/17.

♠ To determine the probability of both of these events occurring sequentially, multiply the probability of each event together.

♣ $1/13 \times 1/17 = 1/221$ which gives you 0.0045 or .45%.

So far we have looked at scenarios where both events must occur. What about scenarios where either event occurring is sufficient? In this case you would add the probabilities together for each event to get the total probability of one of your events occurring. For example, what is the probability of being dealt a single ace?

♣ The probability of getting an ace on the first card and a blank on the second card[2] is $4/52 \times 48/51 = 0.0724$.

♠ The probability of getting a blank on the first card and an ace on the second card is $48/52 \times 4/51 = 0.0724$.

♦ Add these two probabilities together: $.0724 + .0724 = 0.145$ or 14.5%.

♥ Therefore, you will get dealt an ace about once every seven hands $(1/.145 = 6.9)$.

Odds are another way to express probabilities. **Odds** tell you how often an event *will not* occur… "The Atlanta Braves are 2 to 1 to win the World Series." In other words, the Braves should win once if they played the Series three times (unfortunately for Braves fans they have not even done that well). To convert probabilities to odds, simply divide 1 by the probability and then subtract 1. In the Braves example, $1/.33 - 1 = 2$ to 1. Going back to the probability of being dealt a pair of aces, the odds would be $1/.004525 - 1$, which gives us 220 to 1.

The odds can also be calculated by dividing the probability of the event *not* occurring by the probability that it *will* occur. For example, if the Braves have a .33 chance of winning the World Series, they have a .67 (calculated as 1 - .33) chance of losing. .67/.33 gives us 2 to 1. This method basically

---

[2] The "48" in this calculation is simply the 51 remaining cards less the three aces still in the deck.

relates probability to 100. For example, if the probability is .25, the event will occur once out of every four times. Therefore, 3 times it will not occur, making our odds 3 to 1.

Note that the above examples merely offer two different ways to calculate the same thing:
$1/.33 - 1 = 2$ to 1 while $(1-.33)/.33 = 2$ to 1.

Here is a summary of the more common probabilities and how they convert to odds:

Probability	Odds
.50	1 to 1 (even odds)
.40	3 to 2 or 1.5 to 1
.33	2 to 1
.25	3 to 1
.20	4 to 1
.17	5 to 1
.14	6 to 1
.125	7 to 1
.11	8 to 1
.10	9 to 1
.09	10 to 1
.01	99 to 1

Probability Calculations

Before going into some examples we need to understand some basic concepts when discussing Hold'em calculations. It is important to understand what cards are known and what cards are not. For example, before the flop, you know only two cards for certain. On the flop, you now know three more cards for certain. These known cards help determine how many more cards are available to help your hand.

If you know five cards after the flop, then it is easy to see that there are 47 unknown cards. After the turn, there are 46 unknown cards. These are the numbers we use when calculating Hold'em situations. It does not matter that opponents might have already folded their hands into the muck. Some people make the mistake of thinking that their opponents might have mucked some of the cards they need to improve their hand. The problem is that we do not know what they mucked. There still are 47 unknown cards so that is what we base the calculations on.

Calculating probabilities is a rather simple process. We can apply now what we have learned to look at some more advanced scenarios. Once you understand the basic thought processes behind these examples you will be ready to calculate the probability of any different type of scenario that you might think of.

You are dealt AK. What is the probability that you will hit *exactly* one pair on the flop assuming you match your ace or king? There are six different combinations of flops that will give you one pair: Axx, xAx, xxA, Kxx, xKx, xxK. In other words, the first card could be an ace followed by two blanks. The first card could be a blank, the second an ace, and the third a blank. Finally, you could get two blanks and then an ace. The same combinations exist for pairing the king.

Once you know the probability for each, you can just add them together to get the total probability of any of the events occurring. Since the probability will be the same for each combination, a simpler method is to just multiply the probability of one scenario by 6. To start the calculation, first determine the probability of receiving a flop of Axx when you hold AK (the x is not an ace or king and the two x's do not match):

♣ The probability of an ace falling on the first card is 3/50.

♥ The probability of a blank falling on the next card is 44/49. In other words, of the remaining 49 cards, 44 of them are not an ace or king.

♦ The probability of receiving a blank on the last card is then 40/48. Note that the flop cannot contain a pocket pair or you will have two pair. Therefore, there are 40 cards that give you a blank and 8 that do not (2 aces, 3 kings, and 3 cards which match the 2nd card).

♠ 3/50 × 44/49 × 40/48 gives you 0.045 or 4.5%.

♣ The probability for the other combinations like xAx, xxA, Kxx, etc. is the same. Therefore, multiplying .045 × 6 gives you 0.27 or 27% chance of flopping exactly a pair of aces or kings.

Now, consider a scenario quite similar to the one above. Once again you are dealt AK. What is the probability that you will hit one pair *or better* on the flop assuming you match your ace or king?

In this case, once you flop an ace or king you have met the conditions of the scenario. Therefore, the probability is much higher since you are not limited to just one pair as you can also hit two pair, trips, or a full-house. It is easier to work in reverse in this case and just determine the probability of not hitting an ace or king on the flop.

♠ The probability of not flopping an ace or king is 44/50 × 43/49 × 42/48 = 67.6%.

♦ If you do not flop an ace or king 67.6% of the time, you can just subtract from 100% to determine how often you do.

♣ 100% - 67.6% = 32.4% which is about 2 to 1 against occurring.

No wonder it always seems like we never hit a flop with AK! The strength of AK is that when you do hit your hand you will often win. Compare this to hands like 7♠ 5♣ where even if you hit a pair you will often lose. Of course, we have not included the possibilities of straights and flushes. But do not get too excited, you will only flop a straight about .33% of the time. When your hand is suited, you will flop a flush a little less than 1% of time (these calculations are done later in the book).

Consider a different type of example. What is the probability that you will flop at least a set when holding a pocket pair?[3] We will assume your pocket pair is TT.

♣ The best way to calculate these types of problems is to work in reverse. Accordingly, we will calculate the probability of not flopping a T.

♥ $48/50 \times 47/49 \times 46/48 = 0.8824$ or 88%

♦ 100% - 88% = 12%. Therefore, 12% of the time we will flop at least a set.

♠ 12% is 7.5 to 1 against occurring.

This example illustrates why we need a lot of opponents in a pot to play a small pair in limit Hold'em. A big pot is needed to justify the 7.5 to 1 odds against hitting a set.

What is the probability of flopping quads when holding AA?

♥ Determine the number of combinations: AAx, AxA, xAA.

♦ The probability of getting an ace on the first card is 2/50 and on the second card it is 1/49. This gives us 0.0008.

♣ However, the cards can be arranged in 3 different combinations so we multiply this by 3 to get 0.002, which is 407 to 1.

♠ Answer: You will flop quads once every 408 times you are dealt a pocket pair.

If you are dealt a pocket pair once every 17 hands and hit quads once every 408 hands, how often will you flop quads if you play every pair? Simply multiply the probabilities together. $1/17 \times 1/408 = 1/6936$.

Hopefully you are starting to get the idea on how to calculate the probability of the various scenarios that can occur in Hold'em. There are more examples like this in the Charts and Stats section of the book. Once you understand the basic thought processes behind these types of calculations, you will be able to calculate the probabilities for many different scenarios.

If you still are having problems understanding some of these calculations, do not fret too much just yet. The point of this text is to teach you the skill

---

[3] We are assuming that the flop contains at least one card that matches your pair. Full-houses where the board is something like 888 are not included in this calculation.

of applying odds without necessarily doing the exact calculation each time. Some simple memorization is enough to give most players all the information they need in the heat of battle.

Poker Odds Calculators

Mathematical computations can sometimes only take you so far. Poker is a very complex game and we sometimes need to use computer simulators to help us with the calculations. Computer simulators will run scenarios thousands or even millions of times so that we can see what the result would be in the long term.

For example, what are the odds that AQ will beat K5? Trying to calculate this on paper would be a very time consuming task, as there are over a couple hundred thousand different types of possible board combinations to analyze! Computer simulators offer us the means to quickly and efficiently calculate the probabilities for this and similar complex problems.

To help with these types of scenarios, there is a poker odds calculator at my website, www.InternetTexasHoldem.com. You can also access the calculator using the CD that came with this book. The ITH Poker Odds calculator is the most advanced web-based calculator on the Internet. In addition to running common heads-up scenarios, you can run scenarios against random hands or a range of hands.

But I have saved you a lot of work and heartache. The charts in the back of the book represent the most comprehensive set of charts and stats ever put in print for Texas Hold'em. You will not need to do these simulations yourself as most of them are in the back of this book.

Chapter Review

❑ Fractions are one way of expressing probabilities such as "you have a one in three chance of improving." This would be written as 1/3. The numerator is the top number in the fraction or "1" in this example. The denominator is the bottom number or "3" in this example.

❑ To add fractions, you first need to convert the fractions to a common denominator. Once you have a common denominator you simply add the numerators together and place the result over the common denominator.

❑ To multiply fractions, you simply multiply the numerators together to get the new numerator and multiply the denominators together to get the new denominator.

❑ *Probabilities* tell you how often a certain event *will* occur. They are often expressed as a fraction.

❑ To calculate the probability of two or more events occurring sequentially you simply multiply the individual probabilities of each event together.

❑ *Odds* tell you how often an event *will not* occur. To convert probabilities to odds, simply divide 1 by the probability and then subtract 1.

❑ Poker odds calculators help with complex calculations by running scenarios thousands or even millions of times.

Test Your Skills

1/ Your best friend is one of the luckiest people you know. Luck is really on his side now as he has just hit the lottery, which was a 1 in 10 million chance. You decide to give him $1 to play the next lottery for you. What is the probability that he will win again?

Answer: This question is fundamental to probabilities. It is related to the age-old question, "You have flopped heads 10 times in row, what is the chance you will flop heads again?" Previous events have no impact on future events. If you are on a good or bad run of cards, this has no impact on the next hand. The answer is 1 in 10 million.

2/ What is the probability of winning the lottery twice in a row?

Answer: This is a little different than the previous question. You must win twice in a row whereas in the previous question your friend had already won once. The probability of two events occurring consecutively is calculated by multiplying the probability of each event together. In this example, $1/10,000,000 \times 1/10,000,000$ equals $1/100$ trillion. We will not get into how greedy someone would have to be to play the lottery again one week after just winning! 1 in 100,000,000,000,000.

3/ What are the *odds* of looking down at your first card and seeing an ace?

Answer: In this chapter we calculated that the probability of being dealt an ace was 4/52 or 1/13 or 0.077. To convert probabilities to odds you take the inverse and subtract 1. $1/.077 - 1 = 12$ to 1. Thinking logically, there are 13 cards in each suit so 12 of them will come for every ace. The odds against landing an ace for your first card are 12 to 1.

4/ What is the probability that your best friend's birthday resides within the same month as yours?

Answer: Without getting too complicated by looking at how many days are in each month or at scientific explanations of higher fertility dates, the probability is roughly 1/12 that any one person was born within the same month as you. The odds are 11 to 1. The probability is 1/12 or 0.0833.

5/ Your cousin aspires to be David Copperfield and makes you the following offer, "I bet you I can pick the A♥ out of a deck of cards without looking. You owe me $50 if I do it and I owe you $1 if I cannot." Should you take the bet?

Answer: You are giving 50 to 1 odds on a 51 to 1 chance that your cousin picks the card. If you tried this 52 times, you would end up winning $1 on average. Take the bet as long as he is not using a trick deck! Yes.

6/ What are the odds of getting dealt AA twice in a row?

Answer: First we need to determine the probability of getting dealt AA. The probability of receiving an ace on the first card is 4/52. Now there would be 3 aces remaining, or 3/51. Multiply these together to get the probability that both occur consecutively. $4/52 \times 3/51 = 0.0045$. The chance that you would be dealt aces twice in a row is: $.0045 \times .0045 = 0.00002$. Take the inverse and subtract 1 to get 49,383 to 1. About once every 50,000 hands you will have the pleasure of being dealt pocket aces twice in a row. If you are at the final table of the main event of the WSOP when this occurs you have great timing! Of course, you still need them to hold up! 49,383 to 1.

7/ You go to Vegas and decide to play some blackjack with eight decks. You get dealt blackjack[4] and the dealer asks, "Insurance?" Should you take it?

Answer: You should not have to do the math with this question since we all know that the casino would not offer you something if they expected to lose in the long run! Nevertheless, we are looking at the math. When you take insurance, your expectation is equal to your bet. When you do not take insurance, you either win nothing or win 1½ times your bet. About[5] 9 times out of 13 the dealer will not hit blackjack (a T, J, Q, or K is bad while any A-9 is good). 9/13 × 1.5 = 1.04 bets. 1.04 bets are better than just one bet when taking insurance. If you are betting $10, you are giving up $.40 every time you take insurance[6]. Therefore, do not take the insurance.

8/ You hold A♣ K♣. What is the probability of flopping a royal straight flush?

Answer: On the first card, there is a 3/50 chance of hitting one of the needed cards. The next card has a 2/49 chance. You then have a 1/48 chance of finishing your straight flush. 3/50 × 2/49 × 1/48 = 0.00005 or 19,599 to 1.

9/ You hold the T♣ 9♣. What is the probability of flopping a straight flush?

Answer: This is slightly more complex than the previous question. There are four straight flush possibilities: K♣ Q♣ J♣, Q♣ J♣ 8♣, J♣ 8♣ 7♣, and 8♣ 7♣ 6♣. In this case, the probability is simply 4(3/50 × 2/49 × 1/48) = 0.0002 or 4,899 to 1.

---

[4] Blackjack or 21 pays 1 ½ times your bet, but only when the dealer does not have blackjack. If the dealer has blackjack, you win nothing and you lose nothing. The dealer offers insurance whenever he shows an ace. With insurance, you basically elect to just have the dealer pay you the exact amount of the bet and give up your chance of winning 1 ½ times your bet.

[5] I use the word "about" since we could get more technical and make a precise calculation based on the fact that two aces and a face card are known to have already been dealt.

[6] Card counters can sometimes beat these odds and take insurance when they know that there is a higher probability of face cards than normal.

10/ You hold TT and raise before the flop. What is the probability that you will see an unfavorable flop? We will define an unfavorable flop as one where any over-card falls and you do not hit a set.

Answer: We need to first look at the various combinations that can result with an unfavorable flop. The order of the three cards on the flop could be:

* ♣ An over-card, any card other than a T, and any card other than a T
* ♥ No over-card or T, an over-card, any card other than a T
* ♦ No over-card or T, no over-card or T, an over-card

There are sixteen over-cards to a T. Out of the remaining cards in the deck, this gives 16 over-cards, two T's, and 32 under-cards. The entire calculation is done as follows:

$16/50 \times 47/49 \times 46/48 = 0.294$
$32/50 \times 16/49 \times 46/48 = 0.20$
$32/50 \times 31/49 \times 16/48 = 0.135$

Total $= 0.63$ or 63%

Applying Odds and Probabilities in Limit Hold'em

Beginning poker players sometimes follow the advice: bet if you think you have the best hand and fold if you think you have the worst hand. However, there are many situations in poker where you have the correct odds to continue playing in hopes of improving your hand to the winning hand. This is a simple exercise of determining whether the pot is large enough, given the size of the bet, to try and improve your hand. Odds and probabilities can help you determine whether or not you should continue with your hand.

One of the first skills that beginner poker players need to master is the math of drawing to know when they should continue their hand and when they should muck. It basically comes down to whether or not you have a positive or negative expectation by continuing the hand.

The following example shows how you can use math to make good poker decisions. You are playing in a $1-$2 game and are seated on the button. You hold J♣ T♣ and the board shows 9♥ 7♣ A♦ 4♠. To simplify this example, assume that your opponent has at least a pair of aces or better; therefore, you need an 8 to hit a straight to improve to the best hand. Should you call a bet?

- ♥ There are four 8's in the deck and there are 46 cards left that you have not seen. Therefore, there are 42 that will not help you and 4 that will.
- ♦ Divide 42/4 and you get the odds against improving to your straight of 10.5 to 1 or 11 to 1 by rounding up (we will discuss these calculations in more detail later). You will lose almost 11 out of 12 times!

At first glance it appears that this is an easy fold; however, sometimes it is worth taking long shots if the pot is big enough to justify the risk. In this case, since you must risk $2 to see the river card, you can only justify calling if you have the possibility of earning at least $21 (10.5 × $2). If there is more than $21 in the pot you have an easy decision. If there is only $12 in the pot you also have an easy decision since you will not be able to win enough money to justify the risk of 10.5 to 1. If the pot is $20, you might be able to call if you think you can earn at least $2 more on the river should you hit your hand.

We can look at this hand in a different way. You are going to win only once every 12 tries (when rounding to 11 to 1). If you played this hand twelve times, you should expect to lose $2 11 times before you hit your straight. That is a total of $22. Therefore, to justify calling, you need to be able to win at least $22 the time you do hit your straight to justify all those times you end up losing $2.

To better understand how to apply odds, we will first look at some definitions such as pot odds and outs. We will then look at how to calculate the odds against improving for the typical situations in Hold'em. The actual calculation however is not as important as how you *apply* odds to make correct decisions, so we will discuss this process in detail.

Drawing in Limit Hold'em Beginner's Concepts

Definitions

Odds and probabilities are two ways to express the same thing. As we discussed earlier, probabilities tell you how frequently an event *will* happen. For example, you will be dealt a pocket pair once every 17 hands or 5.88% of the time. *Odds* tell you how many times an event *will not* happen. For example, the odds are 16 to 1 against being dealt a pocket pair.

Pot odds is the relationship between the current pot and the current bet. For example, if the pot is $100 and you must call $10, the pot odds are 10 to 1.

An *out* is an important concept when discussing probability and odds. An out is a card that improves your hand. For example, when you hold two hearts and there are two hearts on the board, you need one more heart for a flush. There are nine remaining hearts or "outs" to improve your hand. If you have A♥ T♥ and you think another ace would also win the hand, you now have 12 outs: the nine hearts and the three remaining aces.

Now that we know some definitions we can look at how to calculate the odds of improving your hand.

Calculating the Odds

Key Concept: To determine the odds against improving your hand on the next card, compare the total number of cards that will not help you to the number of cards or "outs" that will.

For example, you hold K♣ 6♣ with a flop of A♣ T♥ 5♣. On the flop there are 47 unseen cards. Out of these 47, there are nine clubs remaining that will improve your hand to a flush and 38 cards that will not; therefore, the odds against improving to a flush are 4.2 to 1 (38/9). An open-ended straight draw has eight outs, which are 4.9 to 1 against improving (39/8). An inside straight draw, a.k.a. a *gut-shot* draw, has four outs, which are 10.75 to 1 (43/4).

If you do not improve on the turn and want to know the odds that the river card will improve your hand, the odds will improve just slightly as one more card in the deck has been seen. There are only 46 unseen cards on the turn; therefore, a flush draw is now 4.1 to 1 (37/9), which is just slightly better than the 4.2 to 1 odds you had when drawing on the flop.

To determine the *probability* of improving on the next card, simply divide your outs by the total number of cards left in the deck. For example, the probability of improving a flush draw to a flush on the next card is 19% (9/47). You will improve to a straight from an open-ended straight draw 17% of the time (8/47), and from a gut-shot straight draw 8.5% of the time (4/47). A lot of people like to know the percentages but I find it easier to know the odds in actual play. When you know the odds are 11 to 1 rather than a percentage like 8.5%, you can compare the odds against improving to the pot odds you are receiving.

This section looked briefly at how to calculate simple odds and probabilities; however, calculating odds in your head during a poker game can be quite cumbersome. In reality, all you need to do is memorize the following table.

One-Card Drawing Table

Number of Outs	Drawing One Card on Flop*
20	1.3 to 1
19	1.5
18	1.6
17	1.8
16	1.9
15 (Flush draw with two over-cards)	2.1
14	2.4
13	2.6
12 (Flush draw with over-card)	3
11	3.3
10	3.7
9 (Flush draw)	4
8 (Open-ended straight draw)	5
7	6
6 (Two over-cards)	7
5	8
4 (Gut-shot draw)	11
3	15
2 (Trying to hit a pocket pair)	23
1	46

* When drawing one card on the turn, the odds are slightly better since one more card has been exposed.

You can see that I am using the odds on the flop of hitting my hand on the next card, even though there is still a turn and river card. I advocate making decisions one street at a time in Limit Hold'em. Calculating the odds with two cards to come and the situations where this is relevant is discussed later in the chapter.

Drawing in Limit Hold'em

Now that we know some definitions and how to calculate the odds against improving our hand, we can proceed with learning how to apply the odds during an actual game. There are several basic steps that you should go through each time you have to draw to improve your hand:

1. Determine the number of outs.
2. Calculate the odds against improving your hand.
3. Calculate the pot odds.
4. Compare the pot odds to the odds against improving your hand.
5. Determine your best strategy.

This is the basic process. We will be looking at a couple of additional steps in the next chapter on Advanced Concepts but we first need to learn the basic steps before moving to more complicated hand examples.

Here are a few examples to show how to apply these steps.

$1-$2 Limit. An early and middle position player both call. You call on the button with K♣ 9♣. The small blind calls, and five players see the flop of A♣ 8♣ 4♦. The small blind bets and everyone folds to you. For purposes of this example, the small blind is the type of player who would never bet a semi-bluff and who would always slow-play a set or two pair; therefore, we assume he has a pair of aces. What should you do?

- ♣ **Determine the number of outs.** You have a flush draw and need another club to improve your hand. There are 13 total clubs in a deck of cards. You have two of those clubs in your hand and two more have flopped. Therefore, there are nine remaining clubs to improve your hand.

- ♦ **Calculate the odds against improving your hand.** There are 47 cards left in the deck. Of the 47, 38 cards will not improve your hand while 9 cards will. The odds against improving are 38/9 or approximately 4 to 1. Remember that the odds chart makes for an easy cheat sheet when calculating odds.

♥ **Calculate the pot odds.** The total pot at this point is $6 (five players paid $1 to see the flop + a $1 bet on flop by the small blind). You face a bet of $1 so your pot odds are 6 to 1.

♠ **Compare the pot odds to the odds against improving your hand.** You are getting 6 to 1 pot odds, which compare favorably to the 4 to 1 odds against improving your hand.

♣ **Determine your best strategy.** You should at least call since calling has a positive expectation. Raising is a consideration to try and buy a free card[7].

$1-$2 Limit. An early player calls and you call on the button with Q♦ T♦. The small blind calls and four players see the flop of A♥ 9♣ 8♠. The same player in the small blind bets out again and once more we assume he has a pair of aces. The big blind and early player fold. What should you do?

♣ **Determine the number of outs.** You have a gut-shot straight draw and need a jack to improve your hand. Therefore, you only have four outs.

♦ **Calculate the odds against improving your hand.** There are 47 cards left in the deck. 43 cards will not improve your hand while 4 cards will. The odds against improving are 43/4 or approximately 11 to 1.

♥ **Calculate the pot odds.** The total pot at this point is $5 (four players paid $1 to see the flop + a $1 bet on flop by the small blind). You face a bet of $1 so your pot odds are 5 to 1.

♠ **Compare the pot odds to the odds against improving your hand.** You are getting 5 to 1 pot odds but are 11 to 1 against improving your hand.

♣ **Determine your best strategy.** You should fold as you have a negative expectation. Note that if you played this hand 12 times, you would only improve your hand once. On average, you would lose $1 11 times for every time that you are able to improve. The problem here is that you will only win $5 when you are able to improve. Based on the pot odds, calling has a negative expectation of $6.

---

[7] Buying free cards is not within the scope of this book. For more discussion on this topic, see my book, Internet Texas Hold'em.

Now, change the scenario in the above example to look at the effect of a large pot. Your hand and the flop stay the same but an early player calls, a middle player calls, you call, and the small blind calls. A crazy maniac who likes to build big pots raises from the big blind. Everyone calls so that now there is $10 in the pot. The small blind bets, the big blind calls, and everyone folds to you. In this case, your pot odds are 12 to 1 while your odds against improving are only 11 to 1. Therefore, calling has a positive expectation because the pot is big enough to justify the odds against improving your hand.

Key Concept: In many cases, it is the size of the pot that determines if drawing to a particular hand is profitable. Given two scenarios where you have the same hand and board, you might fold in one scenario when the pot is small and draw in a different scenario when the pot is large.

This key concept sounds rather simple and obvious, but many weak players play their hands the same way no matter how big the pot is. Weak draws can sometimes be profitable but you usually need a large pot. Get into a habit of always being conscious of the size of the pot. Continue the above example and look at what happens on the turn.

$1-$2 Limit. An early player calls, a middle player calls, and you call on the button with Q♦ T♦. The small blind calls and the big blind raises. Five players see the flop of A♥ 9♣ 8♠. The small blind bets, the big blind calls, and you call. The turn card is the 3♦. The small blind bets and the big blind folds. There is $15 in the pot. What should you do?

- ♣ **Determine the number of outs.** You have a gut-shot straight draw and need a jack to improve your hand. Therefore, you only have four outs.
- ♦ **Calculate the odds against improving your hand.** There are now only 46 cards left in the deck. 42 cards will not improve your hand while 4 cards will. The odds against improving are 42/4, which are 10.5 to 1.
- ♥ **Calculate the pot odds.** With a total pot of $15 and a bet of $2, you are getting 7.5 to 1 pot odds.

♠ **Compare the pot odds to the odds against improving your hand.** You are getting 7.5 to 1 pot odds but are 10.5 to 1 against improving your hand.

♣ **Determine your best strategy.** You should fold as you have a negative expectation. Note how it was profitable to call the flop with your gut-shot given the size of the pot but it now becomes unprofitable when the bets are increased on the turn. If you played this scenario out 12 times, you will lose $2 for every 11 hands played and win $15 once for a negative expectation of -$7. It takes a very large pot to continue a gut-shot straight draw on the turn.

Key Concept: Weak draws are sometimes profitable on the flop given that it only takes a small bet to continue but they are often unprofitable on the turn when the bet amount increases.

Calculating Odds with Two Cards to Come

Sometimes on the flop you want to know the probability that either the turn or river card will improve your hand. These calculations are slightly more complicated. The best way is to multiply the probability of missing on the turn by the probability of missing on the river. For example, for a flush draw you would multiply 38/47 by 37/46, which equals 1406/2162 or 0.6503. Since you will not improve 65% of the time, it is obvious that you will improve 35% of the time. To convert this to odds, invert the percentage and subtract 1 to get 1/.35 -1 = 1.9 to 1 against improving.

flush draw

~ 2 to 1

As we did before, rather than trying to make each of these calculations we can simply summarize them into one chart for easy reference.

Two-Card Drawing Table

Number of Outs	Drawing One Card on Flop	Drawing Two Cards
20	1.3 to 1	.5 to 1
19	1.5	.5
18	1.6	.6
17	1.8	.7
16	1.9	.8
15 (Flush draw with two over-cards)	2.1	.8
14	2.4	1
13	2.6	1.1
12 (Flush draw with over-card)	3	1.2
11	3.3	1.4
10	3.7	1.6
9 (Flush draw)	4	1.9
8 (Open-ended straight draw)	5	2.2
7	6	2.6
6 (Two over-cards)	7	3
5	8	4
4 (Gut-shot draw)	11	5
3	15	7
2 (Trying to hit a pocket pair)	23	11
1	46	23

Before using these charts you need to understand which column is applicable to the decision you are making. Obviously, when you are on the turn you should be using the one card column since there is only one more card to come. On the flop, it becomes a little more complicated.

Many players make the mistake of always making decisions on the flop based on the odds of improving with two cards to come. Do not make this same mistake! The two-card column should be used generally for all-in decisions that are most common in No-Limit Hold'em.

Key Concept: In Limit poker, you should generally be making decisions one street at a time when deciding whether you should draw or not.

The best way to explain this concept is by looking at an example.

You have a gut-shot draw. The odds of improving on the next card are 11 to 1. The odds of improving on either the turn or river are 5 to 1. Players who always call on the flop when they are getting 5 to 1 pot odds are making a mistake.

♥ Many players forget to include the cost of the turn bet. If you are going to draw to the river based on the odds against improving with two cards to come, you must include the cost of the turn bet in your calculation. For example, you have a gut-shot draw in a $1-$2 game and there is $5 in the pot. You are getting 5 to 1 pot odds. Your odds against improving by the river are 5 to 1. If you only consider the $1 bet on the flop then you would call. However, this is incorrect since you will have to pay $1 on the flop and $2 on the turn to see both cards. The 5 to 1 odds against improving are based on seeing two more cards so you *must* include the cost of receiving two cards in your calculation. Therefore, you need to be able to win $15 for calling to be correct ($3 x 5). With only $5 in the pot on the flop, it would be difficult to win the additional $10 from your opponents required to justify a call.

♣ It is often correct to call on the flop and fold on the turn. When using the odds with two cards to come, you will still make mistakes even when you include the cost of the turn bet in your calculation. Sometimes you will fold even though calling one more bet on the flop is correct.

For example, assume that in the above example there is $8 in the pot and you are faced with a $1 bet. If you are using odds with two cards to come, you would again calculate that you need to win $15 in this pot to justify calling. It is doubtful you would win an additional $7 on the turn and river from your opponents so you decide to fold.

But folding is a mistake. On the flop, you only have to pay $1 to see one more card. The odds of improving on the next card are 11 to 1. Therefore, you need to win a total of $11 to justify calling on the *flop*. With $8 in the pot, you are getting pretty good implied odds that you will win an additional $3 on the turn and/or river to justify a single call on the flop (implied pot odds will be discussed more in the next chapter). In this particular example, it is often correct to call on the flop when the bets are small and then fold on the turn when the bets get bigger. Sometimes you eliminate this possibility when using odds with two cards to come.

Note that your position is sometimes important. If you are faced with a bet and there are still opponents behind you, then you might need to fold due to the risk that one or more of your opponents may raise the bet and ruin your odds to draw.

♦ When using odds with two cards to come you sometimes commit yourself to seeing the river no matter what happens. This decision can often be a mistake for a few different reasons. The turn may completely change the context of the board and eliminate some of your outs, or you may face raises from opponents who are yet to act.

How should you make decisions on whether to draw or not when applying odds? In *limit* poker, you should make them one street at a time. On the flop, calculate the odds of improving on the next card and then compare them to the implied pot odds you are receiving. If you do not improve on the turn, go through the same process of comparing the odds of improving on the river to the implied pot odds. When you make decisions one step at a time you will avoid mistakes and avoid over-committing to a pot when the situation might change.

You might ask, "Many poker books offer charts that include two cards to come. When are the odds with two cards to come relevant?" Odds with two cards to come should be used in all-in situations. This occurs frequently in No-Limit poker but is not so common in limit Hold'em. In limit, two card odds are generally only relevant when either you or your opponent might be in an all-in situation because of a small stack. Another application of two card odds is determining whether or not you can raise for value, which we will discuss in the next section.

Remember to be certain to make drawing decisions in limit poker one street at a time and you will be on your way to beating the odds. If you are playing No-Limit Hold'em, then you can begin to use the odds for improving your hand with two cards to come in all-in situations.

Raising Draws for Value

For every rule there is an exception. In the previous section we looked at why you should make decisions on whether or not to draw one street at a time. Once you decide that it is profitable to call, the next decision should be whether or not it would be better to raise.

Key Concept: Sometimes it is more profitable to raise with your strong draws than it is to just call.

Texas Hold'em is a seven-card game. Every hand gives each player two hole cards and a board of five additional community cards. The player with the best hand on the flop does not always have the best chance of winning by the river. Every hand should be evaluated on the probability that you will win the hand by the river.

Key Concept: When the probability that you will win is higher than the percentage of bets you are contributing to the pot, you should choose the strategy that will get as many bets in the pot as possible.

For example, you hold A♣ 5♣ with a flop of Q♣ J♣ 6♦. You have a nut flush draw, which is 2 to 1 against improving by the river. Four opponents call on the flop and it is your turn to act. It is obvious that you should call with this big draw. But consider the value of a raise in this situation. In this particular hand, you will be contributing just 20% of the bets going into the pot and you have about a 33% chance of winning the pot by the river. This is a very profitable situation in the long run! In this case you can raise your draw for value.

Now, consider another example. The same flop comes but this time you hold 8♣ 7♣ and you are up against only one opponent. Your opponent is a rock who never bets unless he has made a hand. In this case, you still have about a 33% chance of winning the hand but you will be contributing 50% of the bets in the pot. Each bet that goes into the pot is now in your opponent's favor. Note that you will still continue with your hand since the amount of money in the pot gives you good pot odds. You would just prefer that all additional bets are kept to a minimum.

We can make some generalizations about raising draws for value. We can see within the chart that you are even money to improve your hand when you have 14 outs with two cards to come. Therefore, each bet that goes into the pot against a lone opponent is a break-even proposition. We would be indifferent as to how many bets go into the pot. Against two or more opponents, we should usually choose the strategy that will maximize the number of bets that go into the pot when we have 14 outs.

When you have 8 or 9 outs such as open-ended straight draws or flush draws, you are about 2 to 1 against improving by the river. Therefore, you are indifferent against two opponents. Against one opponent you would prefer to minimize the number of bets. Against three or more opponents you would prefer to maximize the number of bets. It should be apparent that it is to your advantage to add more bets to the pot when you have a 33% chance of winning the pot but are only contributing 20-25% of the bets.

With 11 or 12 outs, such as an over-card with a flush or straight draw, you would show profits against two or more opponents and would have a small negative expectation against a lone opponent.

Once you decide that it is to your advantage to maximize the number of bets, you must learn the best approach for doing so. With big draws, it is usually to your benefit to keep as many opponents in the pot as possible[8]. Therefore, if you want to keep opponents in the hand you need to be careful when you raise. For example, if the small blind bets and you are in early position with several players left to act behind us, simply calling would be the best strategy as you do not want to force the remaining opponents out of the pot. You might also be careful betting into a pre-flop raiser with many opponents left to act behind him since you risk that player raising and driving out the remaining players.

However, if several opponents have already called then you can consider raising to get them to add another bet to the pot. When we act early, a smart play is to try for a check-raise. This is especially true when the pre-flop raiser acts right behind us. By checking, we allow an opponent to bet and other opponents to follow by calling. Once we get our opponents committed to the pot we can raise. If someone re-raises, we now have the opportunity to cap. Remember, each additional bet that goes into the pot is to our advantage when the probability that we will win the hand is better than the percentage of bets we are putting into the pot.

Learning how to apply math at the poker table helps you know when you should call, when you should fold, and when you can raise. Hopefully these examples help you understand the process. Now it is your turn to test your skills!

---

[8] One exception to this is when the pot is so big that you prefer to drive out opponents to give yourself some other outs such as making your over-cards good.

Chapter Review

❑ One of the first skills that beginner players need to master is the math of drawing to know when they should continue their hand and when they should muck.

❑ *Probability* tells you how many times an event *will* happen while *odds* tell you how many times an event *will not* happen. For example, the odds are 3 to 1 against improving your hand while the probability of improving your hand is .25, 25% or 1 in 4.

❑ *Pot odds* is the relationship between the current pot and the current bet.

❑ An *out* is a card that improves your hand.

❑ To determine the odds against improving your hand on the next card, compare the total number of cards that will not help you to the number of cards or "outs" that will.

❑ The basic steps in applying odds at the poker table for your draws are as follows:
1. Determine the number of outs.
2. Calculate the odds against improving your hand.
3. Calculate the pot odds.
4. Compare the pot odds to the odds against improving your hand.
5. Determine your best strategy.

❑ In many cases, it is the size of the pot that determines if drawing to a particular hand is profitable. Given two scenarios where you have the same hand and board, you might fold in one scenario when the pot is small and draw in a different scenario when the pot is large.

❑ Weak draws, like gut-shot straight draws or a draw when holding bottom pair, are sometimes profitable on the flop given a large pot, but are rarely profitable on the turn where the bets increase. It takes a very large pot to continue a weak draw on the turn.

❑ In Limit poker, you should generally be making decisions one street at a time when deciding whether you should draw or not. Exceptions to this rule include all-in situations from either you or your opponent or when evaluating whether you should raise for value.

❑ When the probability that you will win is higher than the percentage of bets you are contributing to the pot, you should choose the strategy that will get as many bets in the pot as possible.

Test Your Skills

$1-$2 Limit Hold'em.

The under-the-gun player limps in and you call from early position with Q♥ J♥. The button raises, the small blind and big blind call, and five players see the flop of K♠ 9♣ 8♦. Everyone checks to the button who bets. The small blind and big blind both call and the under-the-gun player folds. There is $13 in the pot. What do you do?

Answer: You are getting 13 to 1 pot odds and are closing the betting. You have a gut-shot draw, which is about 11 to 1 against improving. The board is a rainbow so you do not need to worry about flush draws. Four nut outs are 11 to 1 against improving and you are getting 13 to 1 pot odds. Call.

In the actual hand, the player called, missed his draw on the turn and folded.

$0.50-$1 Limit Hold'em.

You are in the big blind with 3♦ 2♠. A middle player limps and the small blind calls. Three players see the flop of Q♦ 6♦ 4♣. The small blind checks and you decide to make a semi-bluff with your gut-shot draw. Both players call and the 7♣ comes on the turn. The small blind bets $1. There is $4 in the pot. What do you do?

Answer: A brief comment on the semi-bluff on the flop. I do not have a problem with this type of play if the players are playing relatively tight. The small blind alrcady checked so it seems that you have a reasonable chance of stealing this pot by betting.

Unfortunately you get two callers so you should not feel too good about your hand. On the turn you are faced with a $1 bet. You have 4 outs requiring a potential pot of $10.50 to justify calling. Given that there is only $4 in the pot this is an easy fold. Also realize that even if you did hit your hand you would lose to anyone holding an 8. There are also flush possibilities that you must worry about. Fold.

In the actual hand the player folded.

$0.50-$1 Limit Hold'em (6-Handed pot).
You are in the small blind with 8♠ 8♦. A middle player limps and the button calls. You call and the big blind raises. The middle player comes to life and re-raises. Everyone calls and 4 players see the flop of T♦ 7♥ 6♣. You check, the big blind checks, and the middle player bets his last $.50. The button calls. There is $7 in the pot. What do you do?

Answer: This is a large pot. You have four solid outs to the gut-shot straight. A gut-shot straight is 10.5 to 1 against improving requiring a pot of $5.25 to justify calling. Given that the pot is already at $7 you have an easy call. Note also that another 8 could potentially give you the winning hand as long as no one has a 9. Another option is to raise. Given that the button called, you have a chance to get the big blind to fold in this large pot. It is possible you have the best hand. The downside to this play is that there is already an all-in player in the hand so you are only protecting against over-cards in the big blind's hand. I like calling with the plan of betting out the turn if the card is favorable. Call.

In the actual hand everyone called the flop and the Q♣ fell on the turn. Everyone checked. The player hit his straight when the 9♦ came on the river.

$0.5-$1 Limit Hold'em.
Two early players, a middle player, and the cutoff limp in. You call with A♥ 9♥ on the button. The small blind calls and seven players see the flop of J♥ 6♠ 3♦. Everyone checks around. The turn card is the 4♥. The big blind bets and a middle player calls. There is $5.50 in the pot. What do you do?

Answer: You are getting 5.5 to 1 pot odds. You have nine strong outs to the nut flush[9]. Your ace and nine might also add a little value to your

---

[9] There is a possibility that an opponent has two pair or a set. In this case, you would have only 7 outs. This is an unlikely scenario given the play of the hand so the correct play is to still call. Discounting outs is discussed in the next chapter.

draw but let us just look at the flush draw. 9 outs are about 4 to 1 against improving and you are getting 5.5 to 1 pot odds making this a good call. Call.

In the actual hand the player called and hit a flush on the river.

$0.5-$1 Limit Hold'em.
You call in early position with K♠ J♠. A middle player calls as well as the button and small blind. Five players see the flop of K♣ J♣ T♦. You bet and the button, small blind, and big blind call. The turn card is the Q♠. The big blind bets. There is $5.50 in the pot. What do you do?

Answer: You are getting 5.5 to 1 pot odds. You have 4 solid outs to a full-house, which are 11 to 1 against improving. If the river is an ace the pot will be split. This is unlikely and would not add much value since you would be splitting the pot with the remaining players anyhow. Even if you count this as one out, you would have five outs, which are 8 to 1 against improving. With pot odds of only 5.5 to 1, this is an easy fold. Fold.

In the actual hand, the player folded and two opponents showed ace high straights.

$0.50-$1 Limit Hold'em.
The cutoff raises, the button calls, and you call in the small blind with A♠ Q♣. Three players see the flop of K♦ J♠ 9♦. You check, the cutoff bets, and the button raises. There is $5 in the pot. What do you do?

Answer: You are getting 5 to 1 pot odds. You have four outs to a gut-shot straight, which are 10.75 to 1 against improving on the next card. Given this board, it is unlikely your ace over-card would add much value to your draw. There is also a chance that the cutoff might re-raise making your draw even more expensive. Given the pot odds of 5 to 1 and the odds against improving your hand of 11 to 1, this is an easy fold. Note also that there are two diamonds on the board. You could hit a T and still lose to a flush. Fold.

In the actual hand the player folded and the T♣ fell on the river completing what would have been a winning hand. Although he would have won, chasing weak draws like this to the river is what we want our opponents to do.

Be sure to evaluate your play based on the odds and not the results. This is italicized as many players try to evaluate their play based on the end of the result of the hand. Always evaluate your play based on the decision you have made rather than whether or not you won the hand.

$1-$2 Limit Hold'em.
A player in middle position and the cutoff call. You raise on the button with A♠ K♠. The big blind calls and four players see the flop of 5♥ 3♠ 2♠. The middle player bets, the cutoff calls and you raise with your nut flush draw, two over-cards, and gut-shot draw. Everyone calls and four players watch the J♣ fall on the turn. The middle player bets, and the cutoff is already all-in. There is $18.50 in the pot. What do you do?

Answer: With this many opponents you should assume that the bettor has at least a pair. You are getting 9.25 to 1 pot odds. Just looking at your nut flush draw, you have nine outs, which are 4 to 1 against improving on the river. With this large pot you have an easy call. Realize that you are almost always getting correct pot odds to call a flush draw on the flop or turn as long as you expect the flush to win. Call.

In the actual hand the player called and hit the nut flush on the river. The betting was great as two other players hit flushes also.

$0.50-$1 Limit Hold'em.
You are in the big blind with A♥ 9♥. An early player posts. Another early player raises. The cutoff re-raises and you make an error by calling. The early player caps it and three players see the flop of 7♥ 6♠ 5♥. You bet, the early player raises, and the cutoff calls. What should you do?

Answer: The pre-flop call is worth discussing briefly. Calling re-raises with Axs will put you in dubious situations even if you are calling from the big blind. Every now and then you will win a big pot when you hit a flush but you will end up paying out a lot of money into a lot of pots if you continually play this type of hand against a re-raise.

But we are focusing on the drawing aspects of this hand. Sometimes we make mistakes that work out in our favor in the short-run. In this case you flop the nut flush draw and a gut-shot straight draw. With 12 outs, you are almost even money to hit your hand by the river. If your ace over-card is good, you are the favorite in the hand. Therefore, with two players paying money on the flop you stand to gain money for each bet that goes into the pot. You have a super draw and should re-raise your hand. Another benefit of re-raising is that the early player might cap it giving the cutoff a reason to fold an ace over-card. Even if he does not fold on the flop, he might do so on the turn and give your ace a better chance for winning on the river. If you do not hit your hand on the turn, you become an underdog (assuming the early player has an over-pair). It then becomes correct to check and call to see the river. Re-raise.

In the actual hand, the 5♠ came on the turn and 9♠ on the river. Everyone checked and the player won with a pair of nines.

$0.50-$1 Limit Hold'em.
A middle player calls and you raise on the button with A♠ J♠. The big blind calls and three players see the flop of K♠ Q♥ 4♠. The big blind bets and the middle player calls. There is $4.25 in the pot. What do you do?

Answer: You have the nut flush draw and the nut gut-shot draw, offering you 12 outs. Counting the ace over-card as a possible out, you are about even money to improve your hand to the winning hand by the river. You are getting 8.5 to 1 pot odds so you have a no-brainer as far as calling is concerned.

The real decision is whether or not you should raise. There are already two callers on the flop, each additional bet that goes into the pot adds positive expectation to your hand given that you are close to even to win this hand by the river. Against two opponents, the "average" hand will win 33% of the time. However, you should expect to win close to 50% of the time. Raise[10].

In the actual hand, the player raised and hit his flush on the turn.

$0.5-$1 Limit Hold'em.
You limp from early position with A♦ 8♦. A middle player calls and the small blind calls. Four players see the flop of Q♣ 7♦ 5♦. The big blind bets. There is $2.50 in the pot. What do you do?

Answer: You have the nut flush draw, an over-card, and a ***backdoor***-straight draw. You are getting 5 to 1 pot odds. Just looking at the flush draw you have nine outs, which are 4 to 1 against improving making this an easy call.

Once you decide that a call is in order, you should evaluate whether a raise would be the better play. In this case you need to weigh the benefits of knocking players out versus the benefits of keeping players in when you hold a good draw. The bettor is in the big blind, and he could easily be betting 2nd pair, 3rd pair, or some type of draw. In this case, you might have two over-cards, the ace and the 8. This makes a compelling argument for a raise to give you a better chance at winning the pot.

However, this pot is not very large. By raising, you may end up knocking out some opponents you would rather have in the pot with such a big draw. The tradeoff with simply calling is that you decrease the probability of winning the $2.50 already in the pot in return for the possibility of winning an even bigger pot by keeping your opponents in the hand. So far, this is a rather close decision but consider one more point.

If you do raise, there still is the possibility that you would get callers. In this case your raise increases your expectation on the hand given at least two opponents. It is a close decision, but ultimately a raise may be the

---

[10] A side benefit of a raise in this situation is that you also might receive a free card on the turn if you do not get any improvement.

best option. Give that you are up against the big blind, an aggressive route that attempts to isolate against the big blind is perhaps the best approach. This strategy also gives you the possibility of taking a free card on the turn or the option of trying a semi-bluff. Finally, even if I do get callers I will not be upset given my big draw. Raising has very few downsides so make the aggressive play. Raise.

In the actual hand, the player raised and three players saw the turn card, which was the 6♠. The player hit the flush on the river and did not get any callers.

$0.25-$0.50 Limit Hold'em.
You just call from middle position with A♦ 7♦. Another middle player raises and only two players see the flop of 7♥ 5♦ 4♦. There is $1.35 in the pot. What do you do?

Answer: This is about one of the best flops you could ask for. You have top pair and a nut flush draw. There is a good chance you have the best hand. The worst play in this situation would be check-calling. When you have a vulnerable pair such as 7's, you want to give your opponent a chance to fold. In this case, betting out could very well get your opponent to fold. On the other hand, this pot is not very large so you would not mind if your opponent happened to be chasing with two over-cards. Given that you have an ace over-card and the nut flush draw, you actually welcome the action. There is a decent chance his outs might not even be good. With such a strong hand, you are not even too concerned at this point of being against an over-pair since you have so many outs to improve your hand.

With this small pot, I prefer check-raising. This gives your opponent a chance to fold, but if he does call, you really do not mind considering this particular board and the size of the pot. If the pot was a little larger I might bet out as this probably gives you the best chance of getting your opponent to fold. Check-raise.

In the actual hand, the player check-called and hit a flush on the turn. His opponent showed AA. Realize that you still had 11 outs in this hand on the flop, which are only a slight underdog. Raising the flop here is only a slightly negative proposition even in the case where your opponent is holding a monster like AA.

$0.5-$1 Limit Hold'em.
You limp from early position with A♣ 9♣. The cutoff raises and the big blind calls. Three players see the flop of 6♣ 5♣ 4♦. The big blind checks. There is $3.25 in the pot. What should you do?

Answer: If you check, the cutoff will most likely bet giving you at least 7.5 to 1 pot odds to call. You would have an easy call with the nut flush draw and two over-cards. The main decision is whether you ought to bet or possibly check-raise. The pot is a decent size given the pre-flop raise with three opponents in the hand. Accordingly, your main goal ought to be to win the pot rather than to make the pot bigger. If you check, it is likely that the cutoff will bet and the big blind will only be facing a single small bet to stay in the pot. However, if you bet and the cutoff raises, the big blind will now face two bets to stay in the pot. You might even get the cutoff to fold if you bet out. Bet and hope a scenario develops where an opponent folds giving you more of a chance for your over-cards to be good. If there is a raise, and both opponents are still in the pot, then you can raise again on the value of your draw. Bet.

In the actual hand the player check-called which is the weakest move one could make in this situation. With a strong draw and over-cards, you need to give your opponent an opportunity to fold. If you are going to check, you need to check-raise and take control of the pot so that your opponent might fold on the flop or turn.

$0.25-$0.50 Limit Hold'em.
An early player limps and a middle player raises. You make a questionable call with A♣ 7♣ from out of position in the small blind. The big blind folds and three players sce the flop of 8♣ 7♥ 4♣. The middle player bets. There is $2 in the pot. What do you do?

Answer: You are getting 8 to 1 pot odds. You have nine outs to the nut flush and possibly five more if you are against an over-pair other than AA or 88. It is also possible that you currently have the best hand. You are going to at least call with this strong hand. There is only one opponent remaining so merely calling will not get extra money into the pot. Raising will possibly knock out the big blind, giving you a better chance to win this decent sized pot if over-cards come. You could very well have the best hand, so raising is the best play to protect your hand. Even if you are against a better hand, you have plenty of outs. Accordingly, raising is not a bad play either way. Raise.

In the actual hand the player called and won the pot on the river when he hit a flush. His opponent showed TT.

$0.25-$0.50 Limit Hold'em.
An early player calls, a middle player, the cutoff, and small blind all call. You are in the big blind with A♣ 8♣ and five players see the flop of 7♣ 6♣ 4♥. The small blind checks and you decide to check. The middle player bets and the cutoff and small blind each call. There is $2 in the pot. What do you do?

Answer: You have nine outs to the nut flush, four outs to a strong straight, and two over-cards. The two over-cards are rather questionable since another 8 could give someone a straight and the kicker on your ace is rather weak. Assuming you just disregard those outs, you still have 12 strong outs, which are almost even money to improve by the river. With three opponents in the pot, you add to your expectation with every bet that goes into the pot. This is an easy check-raise. Raise.

In the actual hand, the player just called and hit his flush on the turn. Although he won the hand the player did not win nearly as much as he should have given the missed opportunity for raising the flop.

$1-$2 Limit Hold'em.
The first middle player raises. The next two players had posted but fold to

the raise. You call from the cutoff with A♦ J♦. The button calls and the small blind re-raises. Four players see the flop of 6♦ 5♠ 2♦. The small blind bets and the middle player folds. There is $16 in the pot. What do you do?

Answer: Nut flush draws are always powerful hands on the flop, especially when there is not a pair on the board. Consider the odds on this hand. You are getting 16 to 1 pot odds! A flush is 4 to 1 against improving on the next card and 2 to 1 against improving by the river. This is a tremendous overlay! Calling is an easy decision. The question becomes whether or not you should raise.

Raising has several benefits in this hand. The pot is quite large so you would like to knock out your opponents and give yourself a chance to win the pot if you hit your over-cards. A raise might force the button player out of the hand. A raise might also buy you a free card on the turn if you do not improve. Finally, with the nut flush draw, your raise has good value as long as you have at least two opponents contributing bets to the pot (since your hand is at least 2 to 1 against improving by the river). Raise.

In the actual hand, the player raised and got a free card on the turn. He got great *action* on the river when both he and the player on the button hit their flushes.

$2-$4 Limit Hold'em.
The under-the-gun player raises and two middle players call. You are on the button and decide to make a weak call with A♠ 6♠. The small blind calls and the big blind goes all-in to $5. Everyone calls and 6 players see the flop of 7♠ 5♥ 4♣. It is checked to the under-the-gun player who bets. The next player in middle position raises and the following player calls. There is $40 in the pot and you face a $4 call. What do you do?

Answer: This is a huge pot offering you 10 to 1 pot odds. You have 8 solid outs although there is the possibility that you might have to split if another player has a 6. You are about 2 to 1 against improving to a straight by the river and the pot is offering 10 to 1 odds making this an easy call. Raising, however, is a better play in this situation.

The pot is quite large so you want to maximize your chances of winning it. By re-raising, you might be able to get the under-the-gun player to fold a hand like AK or AQ. By doing so, you slightly improve your chances of winning this hand should an ace fall on the turn or river.

This raise gives good value even if everyone calls. You are about 2 to 1 to improve by the river so you make money when there are three or more opponents putting money into the pot. By re-raising, you "profit" whether or not the under-the-gun player decides to play or not. Re-raise.

In the actual hand the player called. The 8♥ fell on the turn, giving the player a straight.

$1-$2 Limit Hold'em.
The game is 5-handed. You hold 7♣ 3♣ in the big blind. The cutoff and button both call. The small blind folds and three players see the flop of Q♣ 9♦ 5♣. You check, the cutoff checks, and the button bets. There is $4.50 in the pot. What should you do?

Answer: The best play in this hand would have been to bet out the flop. The worst play is checking and calling which is what this player did. You have a flush draw so you are getting odds to call. However, checking and calling into two opponents gives you no chance of winning the pot. If you are going to call, you might as well bet out hoping that both of your opponents fold. The worst thing that can happen is that an opponent raises costing you an additional bet to draw. Note the risk-return factor from the two different plays. You are only risking one small bet while you have the chance of winning the $3.50 already in the pot by betting out.

In this example, you are going to play to the river. If you do check, it is best to raise the button player in order to get this pot heads-up. By driving out the other opponent, you give yourself a better chance at winning this pot if either a 7 or a 3 comes. You might also force the button player to fold on the turn when you come out betting. In short-handed play, you must play aggressively. There are many hands here where your opponent could have been betting nothing, such as KT, so you need to put your opponents to the test. This is especially true in short-handed games unless you are up against a loose passive player who calls every hand down to the river. Raise.

In the actual hand, the player called the flop, called the turn, and hit his flush on the river. Unfortunately he missed a bet by checking the river.

$5-$10 Limit Hold'em.

The cutoff posts $5. An early player calls and you raise in middle position with A♦ Q♦. The cutoff calls, the big blind calls, and the early player re-raises. Everyone calls. Four players see the flop of 8♦ 5♥ 2♦. The early player bets, you raise, the cutoff re-raises, the big blind folds, and the early player caps it. Everyone calls and three players see the turn of 9♥. The early player bets, you call, the cutoff raises and the early player re-raises[11]. There is $182 in the pot. What should you do?

Answer: You face a $20 call that could very well turn into a $30 call if the cutoff caps it. Therefore, you are getting somewhere between 9 and 7 to 1 pot odds. You have 9 outs, 7 if you are against a set. Assuming worst case, 7 outs are 6 to 1 against improving and you are getting better than 6 to 1 even if it is capped. Accordingly, you should call.

In the actual hand, the player called and the 8♥ fell on the river. The early player showed K♣ K♦ and the cutoff T♦ 9♦.

$3-$6 Limit Hold'em (4-Handed).

You are in the small blind with A♠ 6♠. Everyone limps, the big blind raises, and everyone calls. Four players see the flop of J♣ T♠ 7♠. You check, the big blind bets, and the button raises. There is $33 in the pot. What do you do?

---

[11] When there are a lot of raises on a flop where there are two cards of the same suit, sometimes you should consider the possibility that another opponent has a flush draw also, reducing your outs to the flush. In this particular hand, the raise and re-raise on the turn indicate made hands rather than drawing hands so another flush draw is unlikely.

Answer: You have nine outs with a flush draw which are 4 to 1 against improving on the turn card. The pot is offering better than 5 to 1 pot odds. You also have some backdoor-straight opportunities and the possibility that another ace could win you the pot. This is an easy call.

Another consideration is re-raising. However, you are probably not going to get anyone to fold here. Given two opponents, you really do not have the best scenario to instigate a value raise with your flush draw unless you think an ace over-card might be good. One problem with this hand is that you could hit the flush on the turn only to lose to a full-house on the river. You are acting out of position so I would just call with the 5 to 1 pot odds although it is a close decision between calling and raising. Call.

In the actual hand, the 9♠ came on the turn and the 4♠ on the river.

$3-$6 Limit Hold'em.
An early player calls and you call in middle position with J♠ T♠. Another middle player calls and 4 players see the flop of A♠ K♥ 8♠. The early player bets. There is $16 in the pot. What should do you?

Answer: You have a flush draw and a gut-shot straight draw. It is rare to fold flush draws after the flop. The addition of the gut-shot draw makes this an even more powerful hand. With 12 outs, you are 3 to 1 against improving on the turn and almost even money to improve by the river. There is $16 in the pot giving you a little better than 5 to 1 pot odds. This is an easy call.

The real question here is whether or not you ought to raise. First, consider the flush draw. You are 2 to 1 against improving by the river. Therefore, with each additional bet that goes into the pot, you will break-even against two players (realize that we are disregarding the amount of money in the pot already). Each bet will cost you money against a lone opponent, but you gain additional expectation if you are up against 3 or more opponents. For example, if four players put $1 in the pot (including yourself), an additional $4 is being added. Since you will win 33% of the time, your expectation is $1.33 while you only risk $1. In these cases, you can raise the flop even though you still must improve your hand to win.

In this particular example, you also have a gut-shot draw so you are almost even money against a lone opponent. However, you gain even more expectation against more opponents. Raising might knock out these opponents when you would rather that they stay in the pot. The only reason you might want to raise is to take the pot right away on the flop by discouraging a better with a hand such as QQ. But if this is the case, there is a decent chance that your opponent will check to you on the turn, thereby allowing you to take the pot at that point. Call.

Continuing the example above.
You call on the flop and the next player folds. The big blind raises and the early player calls. There is $28 in the pot. What should you do?

Answer: You are about even money to win this hand and there are two opponents in the pot. Each additional bet from these two opponents adds positive expectation to this hand. Now that you have your opponents in the pot you can go ahead and raise for value. Re-raise.

In the actual hand the player raised and the flop was capped. The 4♠ came on the turn, followed by the Q♠ on the river. The player won with his J♠.

$0.25-$0.50 Limit Hold'em.
An early player and middle player call. You raise from the cutoff with A♥ K♥. The small blind and big blind each call. Five players see the flop of Q♣ J♥ 6♠. The small blind bets and everyone calls the bet making it your turn to act. There is $3.50 in the pot. What do you do?

Answer: You have a gut-shot draw, which is 10.5 to 1 against improving. You are getting 14 to 1 pot odds and are closing the betting. This is an easy call. You can also consider a raise in this situation. You are 5 to 1 against improving by the river and there are four opponents already in the hand. This gives you almost even money on each additional bet that goes into the pot (assuming every opponent calls to the river). Realize also that you have over-cards and a backdoor-flush opportunity. Raising also has an additional benefit - the possibility of buying you a free card. With so many callers, this is a hand where you can be aggressive and raise for value with a relatively weak draw. Raise.

In the actual hand the player called and hit a gut-shot on the turn.

Limit Tournament.
It is late in a tournament and you only have $700 left after posting the big blind. Limits are $500-$1000. An early player and the small blind limp in and you get a free look with 9♣ 6♣. The flop comes T♣ 5♣ 2♦. A very conservative player from the small blind bets $500. There is $2000 in the pot. What do you do?

Answer: If you call, you are pretty much pot-committed since you will only have $200 left. Therefore, you must risk $700 to win at least $2200. This could be more if the early position player calls but on the conservative side your pot odds are 2200/700, or 3 to 1. The odds against improving to a flush by the river are 2 to 1. This is an easy call, especially considering that you need to try to make a move to get back into this tournament. The next question is whether or not to move all-in. It is unlikely that an extra $200 would impact the early player's decision on whether or not to continue his hand, but just in case you might as well raise. You are playing to survive and knocking out the early player just might give you an extra chance to keep alive. For example, a 9 could come allowing you to beat the small blind where you might lose if the early player is holding A9. Go all-in.

Drawing in Limit Hold'em
Advanced Concepts

In the previous section we learned some basic concepts to help us apply odds at the poker table to assist us in making the best decisions. The processes and examples were rather straightforward, as we generally had a very clear idea on all of the information needed to make a good decision. This section will cover some additional concepts to help our decisions when we are faced with incomplete or unclear information. We will have to use our poker knowledge and experience to determine the variables that will go into the odds calculations. Anyone can learn these new concepts and begin to apply them but it will take practical experience before you are able to consistently make accurate determinations about the incomplete information presented to you.

Implied Pot Odds

In the previous chapter we showed that pot odds are nothing more than the relationship between the current pot and the current bet. What really matters, however, is the amount of money you win at the end of the hand. *Implied pot odds* are calculated by comparing the current pot, along with the bets you expect to win from your opponents, to the current bet and expected future bets required to play the hand. You need to include the expected future bets you might make on the turn such as when you are drawing to backdoor-straight and flush draws. Implied pot odds basically take future bets you might win (if you hit your hand) into consideration as you make your decisions.

For example, you are playing in a $1-$2 game and your lone opponent bets out $2 on the turn. There is $10 in the pot, so your pot odds are 5 to 1. However, if you improve your hand on the river, you expect to earn at least one more bet from your opponent. You are risking $2 on the turn to win a total of $12 (the $10 in the current pot plus your opponent's $2 bet on the river). Therefore, your implied odds are 6 to 1. If you expect that your opponent will bet out on the river and call a raise should you improve, you would earn two more bets. In such a case, your implied odds would be 7 to 1.

Note that your risk in the above example is only $2. If you do not hit your hand you will simply fold. The river bet or raise is not included in the calculation since we are assuming that you will win if you hit your draw. In essence, the river bet or raise is a risk-free proposition. Of course, this only happens when you are drawing to the nuts. Sometimes you are unsure whether or not your hand will win even if you improve. In these cases, you must include this added risk into your calculation.

For example, assume that we are drawing to two over-cards. We believe that 50% of the time our hand will win and 50% of the time we will lose (our assumption is that the call is justified based on the money already in the pot). We also assume that our opponent will bet the river and we will call if we improve our hand. In this example, the implied pot odds are break even. Sometimes we will win an extra bet and sometimes we will lose an extra bet. Therefore, we will base our draw solely on the pot odds. If we have a 75% chance of winning, we would be able to add a little more to our implied pot odds.

Another important concept is realizing how much you will have to invest on the current betting round.

Key Concept: When calculating pot odds and implied pot odds, always be aware of the possibility of a raise behind you.

If your bet does not close the betting, you may not be getting the pot odds you expect. For example, an opponent bets $1 and there is $9 in the pot. Your pot odds are 9 to 1. However, if a player behind you raises, you now must pay an additional $1. A raise lowers your pot odds to only 6 to 1 since you will have to pay a total of $2 to win $12[12] (assuming the original bettor calls the raise). There are many situations in Hold'em that require folding when there is a possibility that a raise will decrease the pot odds you are receiving.

---

[12] The total pot would be $14. Your $2 bet is included within that $14 pot and should not be included within the calculation.

Outs versus Douts

Remember that we said an out is a card that improves your hand. However, what we really want to know are the odds against improving to the *winning* hand. This is often unknown, as we do not know exactly what our opponent(s) is holding. For example, we could improve to a straight while our opponent has a flush. We may also improve on the turn only to see our opponent improve to a winning hand on the river. This scenario happens more often than we might think, so we should include its possibility into our calculations.

An out is no good when a card that improves your hand gives an opponent an even better hand. Nor is an out good if your opponent already has a better hand than the one to which you are trying to improve.

Key Concept: One of the most common mistakes made by many players is assuming that they will win when a particular card improves their hand.

For example, you could be hoping for a flush card only to lose to a higher flush or, maybe, even a full-house. You could hit an over-card, only to lose to two pair, three of a kind, a straight, or a flush. There are some more definitions related to this topic.

You are *drawing dead* when you cannot improve to the winning hand. For example, you are drawing dead when holding two over-cards on the turn if an opponent already has a set or two pair, or if your outs would give your opponent an even better hand. This is the worst possible scenario in poker. You are putting additional money into a pot when you have absolutely no chance of winning.

When applying odds, you should *discount* an out whenever there is a chance that the out is no good. Similarly, you should *disregard* the out if you think you are drawing dead. I like to refer to *d*iscounted *outs* as *douts*[13].

---

[13] The term dout was first used by Mike Petriv in his book, *Hold'em Odds Book*. He used the term to refer to an opponent's outs while the term is used here to refer to discounted outs.

A dout is simply a value used to represent a card that improves your hand and then is discounted based on how likely that card would improve you to the best hand. The discounted out or dout can range from 0 to 1.

A dout that has a value of 0 represents a card that improves your hand but has no chance of being the best hand. In other words, you are drawing dead to that card. A dout that has a value of 1 means that the card has no discount since you are drawing to the nuts.

If you are 50% confident that a card will improve you to the winning hand, you would discount your out to .5 of a dout. If you are 75% confident then your out is worth .75 of a dout and so forth.

How much you discount your outs to determine the number of douts is dependent on how many players you are up against and your read on your opponents' possible holdings given the betting sequences in the hand.

For example, you have three outs to an over-card ace and feel that you might win about 2/3 of the time against a lone opponent if you hit the ace. In this case, you would discount your three outs to two douts. However, against two opponents you might feel you will only win about 1/3 of the time, so you discount your three outs to one dout. If you are against three or more opponents, you might feel that even with another ace you have almost no chance of winning. In this case, you should disregard the outs to the ace since you think those outs have practically no chance of winning[14].

Note that on the flop you will need to apply an additional discount for the possibility that when you improve on the turn your opponent(s) will have a chance to improve to a better hand on the river. In fact, there are very few hands on the flop that are draws to the true nuts as your opponents almost always have at least a small possibility of

---

[14] The probabilities of whether or not your ace is good are just used as an example. In actual play, you will need to make your own estimation on how much to discount an out based on the type of opponents you are against and what has happened in the hand up to the point where you need to make a decision.

beating you on the river. For example, you could hit the nut straight or flush on the turn only to see an opponent hit a full-house on the river. The more opponents you are against on the flop, the higher the risk and the bigger the required discount.

After you assign each out a value as a dout, simply add them together to get the total number of douts. *Once you know the number of douts, you can calculate the odds against improving to the winning hand to determine your best strategy.*

The next section goes through several examples to look at how you should determine the number of douts you have in a hand.

Calculating Douts

When applying odds, you need to use the number of douts that could help you improve to the best hand. As discussed previously, it does you no good to improve your hand only to lose to a better hand. Once you know the number of douts you have, you can use the *Out Chart* on page 40 to determine the odds against improving to the winning hand. The following examples will show how to calculate the number of douts.

You hold T♣ 8♣ in an un-raised pot and the flop comes A♣ 9♣ 4♦. An opponent bets. This opponent never slow-plays and will sometimes make semi-bluffs. Therefore, he could have a pair of aces, two pair, a set, or possibly two clubs which are higher than ours.

You still have a strong draw to the flush; however, you must worry about the possibility that your opponent could hit a full-house on either the turn or river. For example, if your opponent has A9, A4, AA (unlikely), 99, or 44, the 4♣ will not help you. Also, any club will not help you if your opponent has any two clubs in his hand with either K♣, Q♣, or J♣. You need to discount your outs for these possibilities. There is also the possibility that your opponent could hit a backdoor-flush if he has the K♣, Q♣, or J♣. None of these are major concerns so you might only discount your nine flush outs down to eight douts.

You have K♦ Q♣ and the board is J♦ T♣ 5♥ 2♠. You have eight outs to the nut straight with any ace or 9 and six outs to the king or queen. The six outs to the king or queen should be discounted since your opponent could already have two pair, a set, or your outs would improve his hand to an even better hand.

In this example, a king would give you a pair but might also give an opponent a straight, two pair, or a pair with a better kicker. Note all the hands you would lose to if a king comes: KK, JJ, TT, 55, 22, AK, AQ, KJ, KT, K5, K2, Q9, JT, J5, J2, T5, and T2. If a queen comes you would lose to QQ, JJ, TT, 55, 22, AK, AQ, K9, QJ, QT, Q5, Q2, JT, J5, J2, T5, T2, and 98.

Key Concept: The degree to which you should discount your outs often depends on how many opponents you are up against.

You have six outs that need discounting in the above example. If, against a lone opponent, you feel that 50% of the time a king or queen will help you win, you should discount the six outs to three douts. In this case, your total douts are eleven, the three douts for your over-card and eight douts to the nut straight. If you are against two opponents, you might estimate that a king or queen would win only once every six times. Therefore, you would have a total of nine douts, eight douts to the straight plus one dout for your over-cards. Against three opponents, you should probably disregard the six outs to the king or queen since there is little chance that you would win. In this case, you would only play if your draw to your eight nut outs is justified.

You have A♣ T♥ and the flop is K♦ T♣ 5♠. All of your outs should be discounted slightly for the possibility that an opponent holds a set. You have two strong outs to the ten, unless an opponent holds KT or T5. Another ace would give you two pair, but your out is no good if an opponent holds AA, AK, or QJ, so you should discount the out to the ace. Finally, you could improve on the turn only to lose to a better hand on the river. Depending on the number of opponents and the betting sequences, you should play this hand as if you had between two and four douts.

You have A♣ 9♥ and the flop is J♦ 9♦ 4♣ with several callers on the flop. You probably are against a flush draw, so the A♦ is most likely no good. You could also lose to another ace if someone has AA or AJ. Always account for the possibility of a set.

Key Concept: Whenever the flop contains two or more cards of the same suit, you should discount any outs of the same suit against a lone opponent and probably disregard the out against several opponents for the risk that one of them holds a flush draw.

A common mistake made by many players is drawing to weak hands when flush draws are likely. As a general rule, most draws are not profitable when the flop contains two cards of the same suit and several callers are in the hand. The only exception to this is when the pot is exceptionally large. This is a key concept since you will be playing with flops that have two or three cards of the same suit 60% of the time! You should always discount or disregard outs with a flop having two or three cards of the same suit.

Another consideration when determining your outs on the flop is the possibility that you could improve on the turn only to see an opponent improve to an even better hand on the river.

Key Concept: Almost every single draw on the flop should be discounted at least a little for the possibility that you could hit your hand on the turn only to see your opponent improve to a better hand on the river.

How much you discount for this possibility depends on the number and type of opponents you are up against, the type of board, and the betting action so far in the hand. There are very few hands that are a lock to win on the turn. Nut flushes can lose to a full-house if the board pairs on the river. The nut straight can lose to a flush on the river. When the flop has two cards of the same suit, the threat that someone might hit a flush on the river is even greater since a likely scenario is that an opponent is on a flush draw.

Most players complain about their bad luck when they improve on the turn only to lose on the river. Good players recognize that these types of situations occur frequently and include this possibility in their decision-making process. If you determine that a draw is close to break-even on the flop, you should probably fold if you have not considered what your opponents might hit on the river. This is one reason why drawing to over-cards, bottom pair, or gut-shot draws can be so expensive. You might hit your draw only to see your hand go down in smoke on the river. Be sure to account for this risk. The looser the game you are playing in, the more important it is to discount your outs for this possibility.

Applying the Odds

Now that we have the complete picture when it comes to calculating outs, douts, and implied pot odds, we need to modify the steps we go through every time we have a drawing hand. First, we need to determine the number of douts. Second, rather than calculate the pot odds we need to calculate the implied pot odds. Therefore, the new steps are as follows:

1. Determine the number of douts.
2. Calculate the odds against improving your hand.
3. Calculate the pot odds.
4. Calculate the *implied* pot odds.
5. Compare the implied pot odds to the odds against improving your hand.
6. Determine your best strategy.

Consider the following examples.

$10-$20 Limit. A middle player calls and you raise from the cutoff with K♣ Q♥. The big blind joins the action and three players see the flop of T♣ 7♦ 5♠. The big blind, a tight rock who never bluffs, bets out and the middle player folds. There is $75 in the pot. What should you do?

♣ **Determine the number of douts.** Assume your opponent has at least a pair since he never bluffs; therefore, you need a king or queen to improve which is six outs. You would be drawing dead against TT,

77, or 55, unless you hit a backdoor-straight. Other likely holdings of your opponent include AT, KT, QT, and JT. In this case, a king or queen would not help against either KT or QT. It is doubtful that your opponent would call a raise pre-flop with K7, K5, Q7, Q5, T7, 75, or T5; therefore, you only need to discount your outs for the probability that your opponent holds KT, QT, TT, 77, or 55.

One other consideration is what could happen if you hit the king or queen on the turn. Your opponent could possibly win on the river by hitting two pair or better. You should discount your outs a little more for this possibility.

To determine how much you should discount your outs, it is helpful to evaluate the probable hands of your opponent. Probable hands that you could beat if you improve include JJ, AT, A7, A5, JTs, and 99. Discounting outs is always a matter of judgment, but you might expect to win this hand 50% of the time when you improve, considering the possibility that your opponent might have a set, KT, QT, or improve on the river. Therefore, you should discount your six outs and play as if you had three douts.

♦ **Calculate the odds against improving your hand.** There are 47 cards left in the deck. We have estimated 3 douts, so on average, 3 cards will improve your hand and 44 will not. The odds against improving are 44/3, which are about 15 to 1.

♥ **Calculate the pot odds.** The total pot at this point is $75 (three players paid $20 to see the flop + $5 small blind + $10 bet on flop by the big blind); therefore, your pot odds are 7.5 to 1 for a $10 bet.

♠ **Calculate the implied pot odds.** Do you expect to win more bets when the king or queen comes? You should win bets 50% of the time when you improve, but you will lose more bets the other 50% of the time when your opponent has a better hand. A simplified assumption would be that all future bets break-even. Therefore, there are no implied pot odds.

♣ **Compare the implied pot odds to the odds against improving your hand.** In this case, we look at the pot odds since the implied odds are the same. The pot odds of 7.5 to 1 are compared to the odds against improving with three douts of 15 to 1 (see out chart).

♦ **Determine your best strategy.** The odds against improving are 15 to 1; therefore, you should fold since the pot odds are only offering 7.5 to 1.

This hand is worth discussing a little further to show the importance of discounting outs. Many players draw to over-cards on the flop hoping to pair up. This example shows that this approach is often a big mistake. If you played your hand thinking you have six outs to the king or queen, your odds are 7 to 1 against improving. These odds compare favorably to the 7.5 to 1 pot odds and you would call, expecting to make a small profit. However, this assumes you would *always* win when the king or queen comes. As we discussed before, your opponent could very well have KT, QT, TT, 77, 55 or beat you on the river. When you take into consideration the estimate of only winning 50% of the time when you improve, this is a clear fold.

Some players also justify calling by saying that they have implied odds of winning more bets should they improve. This is true if your hand wins but sometimes you will lose bets. If your king or queen comes on the turn, you will probably raise and, quite possibly, be faced with a re-raise if your opponent has a set or two pair. Also realize that sometimes when you improve to the best hand your opponents will simply fold. I realize that this does not happen very often in today's Hold'em world but opponents do sometimes fold!

With the K♣ Q♥ and a flop of T♣ 7♦ 5♠, some players would also consider the possibility of a backdoor-straight and call with the idea that any K, Q, or J would be favorable since the J would give them an open-ended straight draw on the turn. Although this possibility does improve the value of your draw, it is only a minor consideration. Backdoor draws will be discussed in more detail in the next section.

$10-$20 Limit. You raise in early position with J♥ J♠. Two middle players, the button, the small blind, and the big blind all call for a total of six players. The flop is T♣ 8♦ 8♥. It is checked to you, and you bet. One middle player, the button, and the small blind call. Four players see the turn card of Q♦. The small blind checks and you bet. The middle position player raises and everybody folds to you. There is $220 in the pot. What do you do?

♣ **Determine the number of douts.** Assuming the middle player is not a tricky opponent, your opponent has at least a pair of queens with a hand like AQ or KQ. He might also have TT, 88, or A8. QQ is unlikely since he probably would have re-raised pre-flop. Q8, J9, and T8 are unlikely since he probably would have folded to a raise before the flop. You have four outs to a straight and two outs to a full-house. Your two outs to the full-house are strong since the only two hands that would beat you are QQ and 88. Your four outs to the straight are relatively strong unless your opponent has QQ, TT, 88, 98, or a backdoor diamond draw. QQ and 88 are unlikely, but TT is a decent possibility. Only a weak player would call a raise pre-flop with 98s. One other small possibility is that your opponent has QJ. In such a case, you would split the pot if a 9 comes. Therefore, I would discount your six outs for a total of five douts to account for QQ, TT, 88, and QJ.

♦ **Calculate the odds against improving your hand.** There are 46 cards left in the deck. We have estimated 5 douts so 41 cards on average will not improve your hand while 5 cards will. The odds against improving are 41/5, which are about 8 to 1.

♥ **Calculate the pot odds.** The total pot is $220 and the bet is $20, so your pot odds are 11 to 1.

♠ **Calculate the implied pot odds.** You should expect to earn another bet on the river if you improve. You might lose two bets on the river if you come out betting with the straight and lose to a full-house. You might estimate that you would win $15 on average when improving; therefore, the implied odds are $235/20, which are 11.75 to 1.

♣ **Compare the implied pot odds to the odds against improving your hand.** 11.75 to 1 implied pot odds compares favorably to the 8 to 1 odds against improving with five douts.

♦ **Determine your best strategy.** Given the large pot, calling is correct.

These examples should give you an idea in how to apply odds during a poker game. In addition, be certain to complete the Test Your Skills section for practice. For beginning players, it will take time and experience before you are comfortable applying these concepts.

Drawing on the Internet versus Live Games

Fortunately, it is easy to calculate pot odds on the Internet since the sites always show the total amount in the pot. In a live game, this becomes more difficult since there is just a big stack of chips in the middle of the table. If you play on the Internet a lot, learn to keep track of the pot on your own so that you will be prepared for when you play in live games.

On the Internet, you have very little time to calculate all of these odds in your head. Here are some simple steps to help you in the heat of the action.

♣ Try memorizing the outs for the most common types of draws. For example, you should automatically know that a flush draw has nine outs, an open-ended straight draw eight outs, and a gut-shot draw is four outs.

♦ Quickly discount your outs and determine the number of douts you have based on the possible holdings of your opponents.

♥ Once you know your douts, simply look at the chart posted next to your computer to determine the odds against improving.

♠ Compare the odds against improving to the implied pot odds.

Keep following these simple steps every time you have a draw and pretty soon you will find yourself going through the steps quite quickly. Once a hand is over, ask the site for a hand history so that you can go back after your session and evaluate your play when you have more time. Look at the actual number of outs you could have won with based on your opponents' hands and see if calling was correct. Keep a log of your mistakes so that you can keep reviewing them to ensure that you do not make the same mistakes in the future.

One other way to practice using these concepts is to study hand examples and recommended plays by top players. Read books that give lots of hand examples to see how the authors explain the scenarios. Another great way to practice is to read and post hands in the poker forum at my website, www.InternetTexasHoldem.com. These can help you see how other players determine outs and probabilities.

The Poker Tutor at my website is also a great way to learn from the pros. The Poker Tutor allows you to watch pros playing in an online setting and gives you the opportunity to read their comments on each play that they make. This application is a great way to see how pros evaluate their draws for both limit and No-Limit. A demo of The Poker Tutor is included in the CD with this book.

Backdoor Draws

A backdoor draw is one in which you need to hit a card on both the turn and the river to improve your hand. For example, you hold A♣ 4♣ and the flop is Q♠ T♣ 6♦. A club on the turn *and* the river would give you a flush or a K *and* a J would give you a straight. Backdoor draws are of little value by themselves, as you rarely are getting sufficient implied pot odds to draw solely on the merits of a backdoor draw. However, sometimes they add just enough value to your hand to draw when you have other outs, such as over-cards or a bottom pair and an over-card.

Backdoor-flush Draws
Backdoor draws by themselves are weak draws. To make a backdoor-flush draw, you first need to hit your suit on the turn, which is 10/47, and then hit it again on the river, which is 9/46. Multiplying these together produces 0.042 or 4.2%, which is about 23 to 1. Those are not very good odds!

Key Concept: Also realize that backdoor draws require you to hit two cards, so you will often need to pay a bet on both the flop and the turn. Therefore, you need even better than 23 to 1 implied pot odds on the flop to justify calling when you include the cost of the turn bet.

Consider a more detailed example.

♣ Assume you are in a $1-$2 game and are faced with a $1 bet on the flop, which will close the betting.

♦ To complete your draw, you will most likely need to call a turn bet, also, so it is important to look at your implied pot odds.

♥ Since you will sometimes be folding on the turn, we can estimate your average risk. You will continue your draw about 20% of the time on the turn (10/47). Therefore, your average total investment is $1 + (0.20 × $2) = $1.40 (the actual investment is slightly higher, since you face the possibility of a raise on the turn).

♠ To justify this investment, you need a pot of approximately 23 × $1.4 which is $32. You should call on the flop only if you expect to win at least $32 (assuming that you have no other draws).

You would need to be in a capped pot pre-flop with several opponents to even have a chance of getting close to a pot that big. These types of pots are extremely rare, and even when they do occur, you will need to be closing the betting or you will run the risk of a raise behind you, given all that action. Realize that whatever limit you are playing, you can use the 32 to 1 implied pot odds that we calculated above as the basis for the number of small bets you need to win to make a backdoor-flush draw. If you were playing $10-$20, you would need an expected pot of $320. In $20-$40, you would need an expected pot of $640, and so forth.

There are times when a backdoor-flush draw can turn a fold into a call, which are discussed later in the chapter, but it is important to realize that there are two different types of backdoor-flush draws, one of which is more valuable than the other:

1. You hold two cards of the same suit in your hand and one hits the flop. For example, you hold A♣ T♣ with a flop of K♣ 7♠ 3♦.
2. You hold one suit in your hand and two of the same suit hit the flop. For example, you hold the A♣ T♠ with a flop of K♣ 7♣ 3♦.

Note how the first is more valuable than the second. In the first scenario, your flush is concealed if you happen to hit it. In many cases, you will be able to get in a nice raise or re-raise on the river.

There are several problems and risks with the second type of backdoor-flush draw, in which you hold only one card of the suit in your hand:

♣ The first problem is that there will be three cards of the same suit on the turn. If one of your opponents hits a flush, there could be some raising and/or reraising, making your draw to the river more expensive.

♦ If you do manage to hit your flush, there will be four cards of the same suit on the river. You are unlikely to get a lot of action unless you are up against a very weak opponent.

♥ Also realize that these types of draws have close to no value unless you are drawing to the nuts or close to it. I would place no value on a draw to the third-best flush when you hold only one card of the suit. Your draw is already 23 to 1 to complete, so you do not want to hit it and lose. For example, you hold Q♣ T♥ and the flop comes 6♣ 3♣ 2♠. Your backdoor draw to the Q♣ is quite weak, given that anyone holding the A♣ or K♣ would beat you. Compare this to the first type of backdoor-flush draw, in which an opponent would need two cards matching the same suit to beat you.

Backdoor-straight Draws

The odds to complete a backdoor-straight draw are not as easy to calculate as it depends on how many gaps your draw contains. For example, you hold QJ with a flop of T54. In this case, you have three consecutive cards without any gaps, so there are several different straight possibilities. Any K or 9 will give you an open-ended draw on the turn. An ace or 8 will give you a gut-shot (note that you will only be able to continue these on the turn with large pots).

Compare this consecutive card draw to a one gapped backdoor draw such as when you hold QJ and the flop comes 954. Now you only have the T to get an open-ended draw. This is four outs less than in the previous example.

The following looks at calculating the odds against completing a backdoor-straight draw with no gaps within it using our first example where we hold QJ and a flop of T54.

- ♣ 16 cards will give us a draw on the turn: any A, K, 9, or 8.
- ♦ We then have either 8 outs in the case of the open-ended or 4 outs in the case of the gut-shot.
- ♥ Since both are equally likely to occur, this is an average of 6 outs.
- ♠ Therefore, $16/47 \times 6/46 = 0.044$ or 4.4%.
- ♣ This scenario is about 22 to 1 against occurring, which is similar to a backdoor-flush draw.

The gapped hand, where we hold QJ and a flop of 954, has even worse odds:

- ♣ 12 cards will give us a draw on the turn: any K, T, or 8.
- ♦ We then have either 8 outs in the case of the open-ended or 4 outs in the case of the gut-shot.
- ♥ However, in this case, the gut-shot draw will occur more frequently. A good way to calculate this probability is to just add the two scenarios for both an open-ended and a gut-shot.
- ♠ An open-ended straight would be $4/47 \times 8/46$.
- ♣ A gut-shot straight would be $8/47 \times 4/46$.

- ♦ $(4/47 \times 8/46) + (8/47 \times 4/46) = 0.029$ or almost 3%.
- ♥ This is about 33 to 1 against occurring.

What about two-gapped hands? Now we are talking about a practically worthless draw. These are about 66 to 1 against occurring $(8/47 \times 4/46)$[15].

Are these types of backdoor draws really that bad? What about hitting trips? If you are not counting a particular over-card as an out, you still have the possibility of hitting trips on your bottom card. For example, going back to the example where we hold A♣ 4♣ and the flop is Q♠ T♣ 6♦, we could hit a 4 on both the turn and river to be pretty happy. The probability of hitting runner-runner trips to one card is $3/47 \times 2/46$, which equals 0.002, or 359 to 1. Well, maybe these draws are that bad!

However, there is one type of backdoor draw that does add some reasonable value to your hand. If you have both a backdoor-flush *and* a backdoor-straight draw, then you now have a draw with some reasonable value. For example, you hold Q♣ T♣ with a flop of J♣ 5♥ 2♠. The odds against completing one of your draws are about the same as completing a gut shot draw with one card. Note, though, that backdoor draws require a bet on the flop and turn. As a result, these types of draws are worth a little less than a gut-shot draw.

When do Backdoor Draws make a Difference?
The best way to think of backdoor draws is to have them be the deciding factor on your borderline draws. For example, you have bottom pair with an ace that you estimate to be 4 douts. The pot is offering you 7 to 1 pot odds and you are 10.75 to 1 against improving. When factoring in the implied pot odds, you have a borderline decision. Once you add in some value for the backdoor-flush you can make the call. Backdoor draws are usually only played as a deciding factor in whether or not you should continue with the hand. Note that these will only impact a decision when the pot is rather large.

---

[15] Note that a backdoor-straight draw to KQJ has the same odds as a one-gapped hand since the ace limits how many straights you can make. A draw to AKQ is like a 2-gapped draw since you can only hit the J and T.

Some people like to think of backdoor draws in terms of outs that they can add to the number of douts they have. Common consensus is to count a backdoor-flush or no-gapped backdoor-straight draw between 1 and 1 ½ outs. If you look at the Outs Chart, one out is about 23 to 1 against hitting by the river. Hitting a backdoor draw offers approximately the same odds. Realize however that this "out" comparison assumes drawing to the river. I advocate thinking of outs in terms of one street at a time. By doing so, you can see that a backdoor draw is worth less than one out. Realize that backdoor draws cost both a flop and turn bet, and sometimes more, so there is a high price in drawing to them.

The bottom line is that a backdoor draw should rarely be played. In cases where the pot is large and you have a borderline draw, a backdoor draw might turn a fold into a call. If you find yourself making a lot of decisions based on backdoor draws, you are probably weighing them too heavily.

Chapter Review

❑ *Implied pot odds* are calculated by comparing the current pot, along with the bets you expect to win from your opponents, to the current bet and expected future bets required to play the hand.

❑ When calculating pot odds and implied pot odds, always be aware of the possibility of a raise behind you.

❑ An out is no good when a card that improves your hand gives an opponent an even better hand. Nor is an out good if your opponent already has a better hand than the one to which you are trying to improve.

❑ One of the most common mistakes made by many players is assuming that they will win when a particular card improves their hand.

❑ You should *discount* an out whenever there is a chance that the out is no good. Similarly, you should *disregard* the out if you think you are drawing dead.

❑ A *dout* is a *d*iscounted *out*. A dout is simply a value used to represent a card that improves your hand and then is discounted based on how likely that card would improve you to the best hand. The discounted out or dout can range from 0 to 1.

❑ Whenever the flop contains two or more cards of the same suit, you should discount any outs of the same suit against a lone opponent and probably disregard the out against several opponents for the risk that one of them holds a flush draw.

❑ Almost every single draw on the flop should be discounted at least a little for the possibility that you could hit your hand on the turn only to see your opponent improve to a better hand on the river.

❑ The basic steps in applying odds at the poker table are as follows:
1. Determine the number douts.
2. Calculate the odds against improving your hand.
3. Calculate the pot odds.
4. Calculate the implied pot odds.
5. Compare the implied pot odds to the odds against improving your hand.
6. Determine your best strategy.

❑ A *backdoor* draw is one where you need to hit a card on both the turn and the river to improve your hand.

❑ Backdoor draws are of little value by themselves, as you rarely are getting sufficient implied pot odds to draw solely on the merits of a backdoor draw. However, sometimes they add just enough value to your hand to draw when you have other outs, such as over-cards or a bottom pair and an over-card.

❑ Backdoor-flush draws require implied pot odds of at least 32 to 1 to justify calling when you have no other outs.

❑ There are two different types of backdoor-flush draws, the first more valuable than the second (see the text for the reasons why):
1. You hold two cards of the same suit in your hand and one hits the flop. For example, you hold A♣ T♣ with a flop of K♣ 7♠ 3♦.
2. You hold one suit in your hand and two of the same suit hit the flop. For example, you hold the A♣ T♠ with a flop of K♣ 7♣ 3♦.

Test Your Skills

$0.50-$1 Limit Hold'em.
 Three middle players call, the cutoff calls, and you call from the small blind with 7♣ 6♠. Six players see the flop of 9♥ 8♥ 4♦. The big blind bets and all three middle players call. There is $5 in the pot. What do you do?

Answer: You have an open-ended straight draw which gives you have eight outs. Given the number of callers on the flop, there is a very good chance that you are up against a flush draw. Therefore, you should discount your outs down to six douts to account for this possibility. There is also the possibility that you could hit the straight only to lose to a better hand on the river. Given the number of callers, I would play this hand as if I had between 5-6 douts. Five douts is 8 to 1 against improving on the next card. You are getting 10 to 1 pot odds so this is a profitable call. A big reason why you are able to call here is that you are closing the betting. Call.

In the actual hand, the player called and the J♥ came on the turn. The player folded after another opponent called a bet. The big blind showed A♥ T♥.

$0.50-$1 Limit Hold'em.
You post $.50 in the cutoff. A middle player limps and you check with J♣ T♦. The small blind calls and 4 players see the flop of A♥ J♠ 7♠. The small blind bets, the big blind folds, and the middle player calls. There is $3 in the pot. What do you do?

Answer: With a bettor and a caller it appears that you do not have the best hand in this situation. You have 5 outs. However, another spade could give someone a flush and a T could give someone a straight. You could also improve your hand only to see that your opponent has a better hand. Therefore, you should discount your outs. I would play the hand as if I had between 3.5 and 4 douts. 4 douts is 10.5 to 1 against improving and requires a potential pot of $5.25 to justify calling. With only $3 in the pot you should fold. Fold.

$0.50-$1 Limit Hold'em.

An early player and middle player both post. The cutoff raises and you call on the button with Q♥ J♥. The big blind calls and both posters call. 5 players see the flop of A♥ 8♣ 6♥. The big blind bets, the first poster calls, and the next poster raises. The pre-flop raiser in the cutoff re-raises to $1.50. There is $8.75 in the pot. What do you do?

Answer: You flopped the 2nd best flush draw giving you 9 solid outs. There are some small discounts to take into consideration. It is possible, although unlikely, that you are up against a king high flush draw. You might also be up against a set or two pair which would decrease your outs. I would play the hand as if I had 8 douts. 8 douts are 5 to 1 against improving. Faced with a $1.50 call, you need a pot of $7.50 to justify calling and there is $8.75 in the pot. Given that you also have implied pot odds, this is an easy call. Even if we discounted down to seven douts you would still be getting good implied pot odds to call.

You could also consider capping the bets here. You are 2 to 1 to improve by the river and three opponents are in the hand. If all nine outs are good, you make money when 3 players are contributing to the pot. The only problem with re-raising is that you might drive out one of the remaining players. You also do not want to add more money to the pot if someone indeed does have a set or a better flush draw. Call.

$0.05-$0.10 Limit Hold'em.

You are seated in the big blind with K♥ 4♦. An early player, middle player, the cutoff, and small blind all call. Five players see the flop of 5♦ 3♦ 3♠. Everyone checks. The turn comes a 6♣ and the small blind bets. There is $.35 in the pot. What should you do?

Answer: You are getting 3.5 to 1 pot odds. You have 8 outs to a straight and 3 outs to the K. First, consider the faulty assumption of thinking all 11 outs are good. In this case, you are 4 to 1 against improving and are only receiving 3.5 to 1 pot odds. But the reality is much worse than this. This board is quite scary against an opponent playing from the small blind. He could already have a straight, full-house, or trips. There are also two diamonds on the board making a flush draw a possibility. In this case, another diamond would not do you any good. All of these possibilities make all 11 of your outs much weaker given the possibility that you are drawing dead. Fold.

Another option is to make a semi-bluff and raise. You might get your opponent to fold the best hand but this is doubtful at these limits. Fold.

In the actual hand the player called and folded on the river when the 3♣ came.

$.25-$.50 Limit Hold'em.
An early player calls, a middle player calls, the next middle player raises, and the cutoff calls. You re-raise on the button with A♥ K♥. The blinds fold, the limpers call, and the raiser decides to cap. 5 players see the flop of 6♠ 6♣ 3♠. The pre-flop raiser bets and the cutoff calls. There is $5.85 in the pot. What do you do?

Answer: This is quite a large pot as you are receiving about 23 to 1 pot odds. This flop is not the best flop for your hand but it is also unlikely to have helped your opponents. There is still the possibility that you currently have the best hand. Your two main worries are that the capper holds a big pocket pair and/or an opponent holds a flush draw leaving some of your outs no good. In either case, you are getting good pot odds to draw to your over-cards. With so much money in the pot, you cannot give up your hand now.

Raising is a strong consideration here. This is a big pot and there is still a chance that you have the best hand. Raising may force out some of the remaining players. Raising might also give you the opportunity for a free card. Raise.

The player called. The 7♠ came on the turn and it was checked around. The 7♦ fell on the river and the player won with her ace. The capper showed Q♦ J♦.

These kinds of hands are tough to play. Sometimes we run into AA or KK and then question our aggressiveness. You simply cannot be seeing ghosts from your opponents all the time and you have to take risks sometimes to be successful in Hold'em. This hand is a good reminder that our opponents do not always have premium pairs when they are super aggressive before the flop.

$1-$2 Limit Hold'em.
The under-the-gun player calls as well as a middle player and the cutoff. You call from the small blind with 6♠ 5♣. Five players see the flop of A♥ 8♠ 7♠. The under-the-gun player bets and the middle player calls. There is $7 in the pot. What do you do?

Answer: There is only the big blind left to act behind you so the probability of a raise is low. There are two spades on the board so you need to discount your outs for the probability that an opponent holds a flush draw, set, or two pair. I would discount my outs to around six douts, which are 7 to 1 against improving. You are getting 7 to 1 pot odds so this is a good call given that you will probably win some additional bets if you hit your hand, especially given that there is an ace on the board. Call.

Raising in this situation out of position with two cards of the same suit on the board is not recommended.

Continuation of the above hand.
The player called the flop as did the big blind. The turn card was the 7♦. The under-the-gun player bet and the middle player called. There is now $13 in the pot. What do you do?

Answer: The board is now paired making it possible that you are drawing dead. This is unlikely given the action so far, although one opponent might be holding 88 or A7. You are getting 6.5 to 1 pot odds and you have 6 douts, which are 7 to 1 against improving. If you hit your hand, you ought to win at least one more big bet giving you the implied pot odds to play this draw. Of course, you might also hit your hand and lose a bet or two. This is a close decision, but I would call. Call.

In the actual hand, the player completed a straight on the river. Note that the middle player showed AQ. If he had showed more aggression and raised pre-flop, on the flop, or on the turn, our hero would not have had the correct pot odds to call. The middle player's passive play cost him this pot.

$0.25-$0.50 Limit Hold'em.
You are in the big blind with T♣ 8♦. An early player, middle player, cutoff, button, and small blind all call. 6 players see the flop of J♣ 9♥ 5♣. The early player bets, the middle player raises, the cutoff calls, the button re-raises, and the small blind folds. There is $3.50 in the pot. What should you do?

Answer: You face a $.75 bet with $3.50 in the pot giving you almost 5 to 1 pot odds. You have 8 outs, which are 5 to 1 against improving. However, you are facing a lot of action. It is quite likely that you are up against a flush draw, which makes two of your outs no good. With all of this action, you should also consider that a set or two pair are also decent possibilities from your opponents. You could hit your straight only to see an opponent hit a flush or full-house on the river. This requires further discounts. Add in the possibility that the early player might cap the betting, thereby lowering your pot odds even further. Fold.

In the actual hand, the player folded. The T♠ came on the turn and the river was the T♦. The middle player showed J♦ 8♥ and the button K♣ K♠. The button won $7.25.

$0.5-$1 Limit Hold'em.
An early player calls, a middle player had posted, and you raise in the cutoff with K♥ Q♠. The button calls and the big blind re-raises. The middle player folds and everyone else calls. 4 players see the flop of J♥ 9♦ 5♦. The big blind bets, the early player calls, and you call. The button raises, the big blind re-raises, and the early player calls. There is $11.25 in the pot. What should you do?

Answer: You are getting a little over 11 to 1 pot odds making this a huge pot. You have 4 outs to a straight and 6 over-card outs. On the surface, this appears like an easy call. However, your outs to the over-cards have little value. Whenever the big blind re-raises, it nearly always suggests that you are up against a big pair such as AA or KK. In some cases you might be facing AK, QQ, or JJ but many players would just call with those hands at these limits. All you can hope for with your over-cards is that you have two outs against AK or two outs against QQ (note that the K♦ or Q♦ is probably no help).

This is not the ideal situation. Most of the time, your opponent will hold AA or KK. Sometimes, however, he might be holding AK or QQ. If you hit a K or Q, you will face yet another dubious situation that you would rather avoid. I would disregard all of my over-card outs (maybe one could argue they are worth .5 outs).

You also have 4 outs to a straight but it appears that you are against a flush draw in this hand. In this case, you need to discount your 4 outs down to 3 douts. Remember that you could improve on the turn only to run into a full-house or flush on the river. In such a case, those douts are weakened even further. 3 douts are 15 to 1 against improving. Finally, there is a good chance that the pot will be capped behind you, thereby lowering your pot odds even more. Given all this action, a fold is your best play. If, based on your reads on your opponents, you decide to give a little value to your over-cards, you may be able to justify a "borderline" call. Such a scenario would be very rare. Fold.

In the actual hand, the player folded and the button capped. The turn brought the T♥ and the river showed the 7♠. The big blind showed Q♦ Q♥, the early player K♦ T♣, and the button took down a pot of $24.25 with A♦ 8♦. As it turns out, the player had 5 outs and a profitable call, but we do not always know this when evaluating all of the possibilities. Be careful in evaluating your decisions based on the end results rather than the known factors at hand.

$1-$2 Limit Hold'em.
The first four players limp into the pot and you hold K♥ 8♥ in middle position. You decide to call. The next player raises and the cutoff re-raises. Such action suggests quite a fun game! The button and small blind show some restraint and fold but the big blind cannot resist the call. Everyone calls and 8 players see the flop of A♥ 5♥ 3♠. The under-the-gun player bets and the next player raises. The next two players call. There is $31.50 in the pot. What do you do?

Answer: You have the nut flush draw. As a starting point for evaluating this hand, consider the worst-case scenario. There is the possibility that the pot might be capped on this flop, which will cost you $4. If someone has a set, the 3♥ will be no good. If someone else has a flush draw, two more outs become unavailable. Therefore, the worst case is that you have six douts, which are 7 to 1 against improving. If the pot is capped, you would need a pot of at least $28 to justify a call. Even in the worst-case scenario you have an easy call.

The next question becomes whether or not a raise would be a better play. There are already four callers in the hand and the pre-flop raisers have not even acted yet! Even in the worst case, you are still about 3 to 1 to improve to the best hand by the river and 2 to 1 if you have clean outs. With 3 to 1 odds, you can raise for value as long as you are putting in less than 25% of the bets in the pot. With four callers you have the players you need to make this a profitable value raise. However, there are still some other considerations.

If you raise, would you be knocking out players behind you who would have called for two bets? There does not appear to be any benefit to knocking out the remaining opponents since you are going to have to improve your hand to win the pot. Each additional player in the pot gives you better implied pot odds. Most opponents will chase this large pot for two bets, but three bets will probably force the really weak hands to fold.

For example, some players might call two bets with a backdoor-straight or flush draw. These players, however, will not impact your hand at all. Opponents holding pocket pairs like KK or QQ might call here for two bets, but may consider three bets to be a stretch (this could potentially cost you the pot on the river if they hit a set on the turn and then the river pairs the board).

At this point, stop and think about your main goal. The best scenario, given your hand, is to have a capped pot with as many callers as possible. By smooth-calling, you have a better chance of keeping players in the hand and there is still a very good chance that someone else might re-raise. Once an opponent re-raises, you will now be able to cap it once the action gets back to you. I think the chance of a capped pot is better by smooth-calling rather than re-raising since some opponents may back away from their aggression if someone else shows strength. Call, although raising is a good option also.

In the actual hand, the player re-raised and five players saw the turn card of a 2♦. It was 3-bet before it got to the player who decided to call based on the odds of hitting his flush. The player rejoiced as the 7♥ fell on the river and he won a pot of $89.50.

$1-$2 Limit Hold'em.
Two early players limp and you merely call from middle position with A♠ Q♠ (a raise is recommended in this situation). The cutoff raises and 4 players see the flop of 9♠ 6♦ 2♣. The first early player checks and the next early player bets. There is $10.50 in the pot. What do you do?

Answer: You have two over-cards and a backdoor-flush draw. There are several problems with this hand. A player has bet into you and the initial raiser. This player most likely has A9, A6, A2, or a middle pocket pair. A set is another possibility if he is a tricky opponent. In the case of Ax, you will only be drawing to three outs to the queen.

The pre-flop raiser also acts behind you. He most likely has a big pocket pair or a hand like Ax. In the case of a big pocket pair you will most likely be faced with a raise. In the case of Ax, you could easily be against AK. Even if you could get him to fold AK, one of your outs to try and beat the original bettor is gone. You are sandwiched between two players who have shown strength. Such scenarios do not offer a good opportunity for chasing weak draws. Fold.

In the actual hand, the player called and the cutoff raised. The Q♥ fell on the turn and the T♥ on the river. The cutoff showed J♠ J♣.

$1-$2 Limit Hold'em.
You limp under-the-gun with A♣ Q♥. Three players call in middle position. The small blind raises, the big blind calls, and everyone else also calls. Six players see the flop of 7♣ 4♠ 2♣. The small blind bets and the big blind calls. There is $14 in the pot. What do you do?

Answer: You have two over-cards and a backdoor-flush draw. You only want to play these hands when you can see a draw cheaply. Although the pot is quite large, there are still three players left behind you who could raise the pot. With so many players involved in this hand, you risk needing to pay extra bets on a fairly weak draw. Fold.

In the actual hand, the player called. The 9♣ fell on the turn and the Q♠ on the river. The player lost his top pair against 9♠ 9♥ from the big blind.

$1-$2 Limit Hold'em.
An early player raises. Three middle players call. You call on the button with K♦ T♦. The big blind calls and 6 players see the flop of 6♥ 4♣ 2♦.

The early player bets and all three middle players call. There is $16.50 in the pot. What do you do?

Answer: You have two over-cards and a backdoor-flush draw. You are facing a pre-flop raiser and three cold-callers giving you a weak draw to your over-cards. There is a good chance your over-cards are no good against so many callers. I would discount the six outs down to two douts.

The backdoor-flush draw is a good draw here since there are no pairs on the board. Two douts are about 23 to 1 and three douts would be about 15 to 1. The pot is offering more than 16 to 1 to call. There is only one player left to act so the chance of a raise is not very high. All of the criteria are in place to make a call here: the pot is very large, it is unlikely the pot will be raised, you have position on your opponents, and your backdoor draw is close to the nuts. Given the number of opponents in this hand, you have fairly good implied odds. Accordingly, and based on the additional value given to my over-cards by the backdoor-flush draw, I would call. Call.

In the actual hand, the player called. The 8♦ fell on the turn and the K♥ on the river. The early player showed A♣ Q♥ and the player took home a nice pot.

$2-$4 Limit Hold'em.
A middle player limps and the cutoff had posted. You raise on the button with A♣ Q♣. The small blind and middle player call. Three players see the flop of 9♠ 5♥ 3♣. The small blind bets and the middle player calls. There is $20 in the pot. What do you do?

Answer: This is a scenario when you can consider calling with a weak draw since you are closing the betting. The flop is a rainbow, which makes it more likely that your over-cards outs are good. Your main worry is an opponent holding a hand like A9, A5, or A3. Since the small blind bet out, he appears to be protecting a hand so it is unlikely that he is playing a set. The middle player could be slow-playing a big hand.

I would discount your six outs to the over-cards to around 3 or 4 douts. In such cases you are about 13 to 1 against improving. You are being offered 10 to 1 pot odds. With over-cards, you never know if you will gain additional bets or lose them if you hit your hand. This can eliminate the implied pot odds or reduce them considerably. I would put the implied pot odds at 11 to 1. This makes the decision pretty close based on your over-cards.

However, you have drawing opportunities for a backdoor-straight as well as a backdoor-flush. These additional draws give you good enough odds to play your hand.

Once you decide to play a hand you should consider whether calling or raising is the best play. In this case, you indicated strength before the flop by raising. The small blind seems to have a decent but vulnerable hand. There is a decent chance that you could win a free card by raising in this situation. If your opponent is not too aggressive, I would try for a free card. If your opponent is very aggressive, then I would lean toward calling. Raise (smooth-calling is a close second).

In the actual hand, the player called. The T♣ came on the turn and the J♣ on the river, completing his backdoor-flush draw. His opponent folded to a raise on the river.

$2-$4 Limit Hold'em.

An early player calls, a middle player calls, and the next middle player raises. The button and small blind both call. You call in the big blind with A♦ 4♦. Six players see the flop of K♦ T♠ 9♥. The pre-flop raiser bets and the button and small blind call. There is $30 in the pot. What do you do?

Answer: This is a tricky flop as there are a lot of high cards on the board. You could be against a set, two pair, or a straight. There are two remaining opponents who could raise the pot. Your backdoor-flush draw is 23 to 1 against improving. Realize, however, that you need to discount your outs a little with this flop given the possibility of someone else improving to a full-house. The pot is only offering 15 to 1 pot odds. You will have to gain a decent number of bets to close this gap. You really do not have any other draws. The backdoor-straight draw is a possibility, but in such case, you could easily end up splitting the pot. Your draw to an over-card ace is quite weak given this flop. This is an easy fold. You are not closing the betting, you risk an expensive draw with the potential of raises on the turn with this type of board, you do not have any other draws beyond your backdoor-flush, and the pot is not large enough in the first place to merit that sole backdoor draw. Fold.

In the actual hand the player called. The turn brought the 7♦ and the river surfaced the 8♦. The player won a pot of 14.5 big bets with his backdoor-flush by gaining an additional $16 on the turn and river. Note that, although he won $46, calling was not justified given that he had to risk $2 on the flop and another $4 on the turn to complete a draw that was 23 to 1 against improving. He also had the ideal situation once he called. None of his opponents raised the flop after him and the board did not pair. This player was "lucky" that his draw did not cost him more. Despite his short-term luck in this instance, the decision will have a negative expectation in the long run. In other words, this particular pot will still not make up for all of the times when luck does not land on his doorstep. Folding was still the best play.

$2-$4 Limit Hold'em.
A middle player calls and the next middle player raises. The small blind calls and you call with Q♦ T♦ from the big blind. Four players see the flop of 9♠ 3♥ 3♦. The pre-flop raiser bets and the small blind folds. There is $18 in the pot. What do you do?

Answer: The fewer opponents you face, the stronger your over-card draw becomes. With fewer opponents, your over-card outs are more likely to be good since you are less likely to be up against an opponent with a monster hand. This is a very innocent flop, one that is unlikely to help your opponent. You are getting 9 to 1 pot odds to call. Your opponent could be holding a big pocket pair, two over-cards like AK, or a middle pocket pair. Looking at the chart on page 180, we realize that there is less than a 50% chance we are against a big pocket pair. I would discount the six outs to my over-cards down to three douts. 3 douts is 15 to 1 and you are only getting 9 to 1 pot odds.

However, you also have a backdoor-flush draw and a backdoor-straight draw. Any diamond, any Q, any J, or any T will complete your draw. Simultaneously, the A♦, K♦, or the 8♦ would also have added value as they give you a gut-shot draw. This gives you a total of 18 cards that would either give you a decent hand or a good draw. With 18 helpful cards, there is a good probability you will either have a pair or a strong draw on the turn. Given a decent sized pot, I would take one more card and see what develops. For those who like to think in terms of number of outs, if we count your backdoor draws as 2 douts and your over-card outs as 3 douts, you have a total of 5 douts, which are 8 to 1 against improving. Call.

In the actual hand, the player called with his two over-cards and backdoor draw. The turn brought the 5♠ and the player folded.

$1-$2 Limit Hold'em.
The under-the-gun player raises and the next player calls. You act next and make a questionable call with A♥ J♥. The cutoff had posted but folds. Three players see the flop of 9♣ 4♠ 4♥. The under-the-gun player bets. The next player folds. There is $9.50 in the pot. What do you do?

Answer: You have two over-cards and a backdoor-flush draw. However, you could be against AA, AK or AQ making your outs to the ace no good or you could be against AA, KK, QQ, or JJ, which would make your outs to the J no good. I always value ace over-cards less than other high cards, especially against a pre-flop raiser who could easily be holding an ace with a better kicker. One problem with drawing to these outs is that you will be unsure, in either case, of your hand's strength. Calling pre-flop raises with weak hands puts you in precarious situations that are actually quite easy to avoid. At best, you can only count your over-cards as three douts.

The backdoor-flush is also not as strong since there is a pair on the board. If your opponent holds a pocket pair then some of your flush outs will not be any good. Three douts are 15 to 1 and you are getting 9.5 to 1 pot odds. The question becomes whether or not your backdoor draw adds enough value to your hand.

Based on this analysis you could make a reasonable argument for a call if you have implied pot odds. However, in this example you are unsure whether or not your over-cards would even win. This is also true for your backdoor draw. You will frequently hit your hand only to lose more money to the pre-flop raiser. Since this could work either way, I would not put any value on the implied pot odds. Although the size of the pot offers a close call, I would fold. Fold.

In the actual hand, the player called and a 3♥ came on the turn giving him a flush draw. The river completed the flush as a 5♥ fell. The under-the-gun player called the raise with T♥ T♠.

$5-$10 Limit Hold'em.
An early player raises under-the-gun. Three middle players call and the cutoff, who had posted, calls. You make a questionable call from the small blind with 5♥ 3♥. Six players see the flop of A♠ K♥ T♠. The pre-flop raiser bets and the remaining players call. There is $90 in the pot. What do you do?

Answer: You have a backdoor-flush draw, a backdoor-straight draw, and are receiving 18 to 1 pot odds. You are 17 to 1 against improving to one of your backdoor draws. The calculation is as follows:

- ♥ Of the hearts that might come, there are 8 that would not give us an opportunity for a straight. When one of these hearts falls, there are 9 hearts remaining in the deck. This probability is $8/47 \times 9/46 = 0.0333$

- ♦ There are 2 hearts that would give us a straight opportunity also. When one of these fall, there are 9 hearts remaining and 3 outs for the straight. This probability is $2/47 \times 12/46 = 0.0111$

♠ There are six non-heart cards that would give us a straight opportunity on the turn. When one of these falls, there are 4 cards remaining to improve to the straight. This probability is $6/47 \times 4/46 = 0.0111$

♣ Add these probabilities together to get 0.0555, which is 17 to 1.

When looking at implied pot odds, you are faced with a \$5 bet on the flop and about 1/3 of the time you will pay an additional \$10. Therefore, your average cost is \$8. $17 \times 8 = \$136$. You need a pot of about \$136 to justify a call (assuming there is no raise).

Consider a scenario where you will pick up four additional big bets on the turn and two more on the river. This is an additional \$60 making your implied pot odds \$150/8, which is about 19 to 1.

You are 17 to 1 against improving so it looks like you can make a call here. However, there are two big problems so far with the analysis. You are not drawing to the nuts in either case. With so many opponents, you need to discount your outs. The backdoor-straight draw needs to discounted since it is likely that someone is on a flush draw and it is possible that someone already holds an ace high straight. The backdoor-flush draw needs to be discounted since an opponent could make a full-house or you could be against a higher flush draw than your 5 high.

Finally, the turn could cost you more than one big bet to draw. This is a decent possibility given the number of opponents in the hand and the size of the pot. What looked like a close call now becomes an easy fold once you discount your draw and account for the possibility of a raise on the turn. As has been stated, it is quite rare to find an example where you can draw solely on the merits of a backdoor draw. Fold.

In the actual hand, the pre-flop raiser showed AK and the player hit a backdoor-flush to take home a nice pot. Let your opponents make these kinds of draws and when they hit, remind yourself that they contribute extra dollars to the pot 17 out of 18 times when you will most likely win.

Applying Odds and Probabilities in No-Limit Hold'em

No-limit Hold'em is THE game today. No-limit has always been the focus for major tournaments, but now even cash games are quite popular. No-Limit Hold'em is not that mysterious when you break down the skills needed to be successful. Basically, there are three key skills needed to be successful at No-Limit Hold'em:

1/ Know your opponents
2/ Know when to bet, call, raise, or fold and
3/ Know how much to bet

These three skills sound easy enough to at least remember, but mastering them requires a lot of experience and study. I doubt if any player in the world feels as though he has completely mastered the game. This next section is going to look at how odds and probabilities can be applied to help improve your results in knowing when to bet, call, raise, or fold and in knowing how much to bet. Knowing your opponent is a topic for another book.

Knowing when to call, fold, or raise draws is always a critical decision in No-Limit Hold'em. The main difference between drawing in No-Limit compared to Limit is that implied odds become a much more important factor. In Limit Hold'em you are limited to how much you can bet while in No-Limit you can potentially win your opponent's entire stack. For this reason the implied pot odds are much higher. Hitting a miracle card can reap huge benefits in No-Limit Hold'em. Conversely, you should make your opponents pay if they want to draw to a long shot.

We will also use some of the same concepts we learned for drawing in Limit Hold'em and apply them to help us determine how much we ought to bet in No-Limit. This becomes critical when you need to protect a good hand. Related to this same concept is the impact of stack sizes on decisions you will face quite frequently in No-Limit, especially in tournament situations. Odds and probabilities help make all of these decisions much easier.

Drawing in No-Limit Hold'em

Drawing in No-Limit is an interesting contrast to drawing in Limit Hold'em. Sometimes you have an incredible amount of implied odds in No-Limit while at other times there are no implied pot odds. If your opponent bets an amount that is relatively small compared to the pot and both of your stack sizes, you have very high implied pot odds. On the other hand, if your opponent bets an amount that effectively puts either of you all-in, there are no implied pot odds since you only win what is in the pot.

In the early and middle stages of tournaments, No-Limit strategy is often centered on implied pot odds - the goal is to win your opponent's entire stack if possible. In the later stages of a tournament, players are frequently forced into all-in situations when the blinds represent a high percentage of their stack. For this reason, it is important to understand the odds for heads-up situations before the flop and for situations where you must commit all of your chips with two cards to come. This explains why we apply odds with two cards to come much more frequently in No-Limit than Limit. We will look first at all-in situations and then at situations where implied pot odds will have an impact on your draws.

Drawing in All-in Situations

Your opponent can put you all-in before the flop, on the flop, or on the turn, when your hand most likely needs improvement. Sometimes you will be getting the correct odds to call even though you are behind. All three of these situations require a slightly different understanding of odds to make the right decision. Obviously, if you think you have the best hand you are most likely going to call. This section is going to focus on those situations where you are likely behind and you have to make a decision on whether or not to call.

Pre-flop versus a Range of Hands

No-Limit tournaments put you into a lot of different situations that require decisions you normally would not face in a cash game. For example, sometimes either you or your opponent has a small number of chips. In a cash game you always have the opportunity to re-buy, so you should not be playing short on chips very often. The increasing blinds in a tournament also become critically important in the later stages of a tournament and can sometimes represent a very high percentage of your stack. For these two reasons, you are sometimes forced to make an all-in decision in No-Limit when you are most likely behind and need to improve to win. Knowing the odds can help us make better decisions.

We can start by referencing the all-in charts starting on page 202. There are two types of charts we will use. The first set of charts look at how a hand stacks up against all other hands. The second set looks at how a hand would do against a random hand in a showdown.

The first set of charts is helpful when you are able to put your opponent on a certain range of hands. For example, assume that a particular opponent would only raise in a certain situation with two cards AQ or higher, AJs, or a pocket pair of tens or higher. By putting your opponent on a range of hands, you can now calculate the probability of your hand winning against that particular range of hands.

To do this, first determine the total number of possible card combinations your opponent could be holding. There are six possible card combinations for any pair (A♥ A♣, A♥ A♦, A♥ A♠, A♣ A♦, A♣ A♠, A♦ A♠) and 16 combinations for any unpaired cards such as AK (a suited hand has 4 possible combinations). Once you know the total number of hand combinations within the range of hands you can calculate the probability of your opponent holding each individual hand. The next step looks at how often your hand would win against each particular hand.

For example, if your hand is 88, you would win about 54% of the time versus all combinations of AK. Now multiply this by the probability that your opponent is holding AK. Once you add up all the different scenarios, you arrive at a 38% chance of winning should you call. Whether or not you call is now a simple exercise of the pot odds in relation to the bet.

The total number of combinations for this particular example would be:

	Combinations	Probability[16]	App. Win % for 88	Totals
AA	6	.09	.195	.018
KK	6	.09	.19	.017
QQ	6	.09	.19	.017
JJ	6	.09	.19	.017
TT	6	.09	.18	.016
AK[17]	16	.24	.54	.13
AQ	16	.24	.55	.13
AJs	4	.06	.53	.03
Total	66			.38 or 38%

Now assume that your opponent will play AA-TT, AK-AJ, and KQs. This adds another 16 possible card combinations that your opponent could be holding. This effectively reduces the percentage of hands opposing you with pocket pairs. Accordingly, your winning percentage will go up slightly to 41%. The calculation is as follows:

---

[16] This probability is calculated by taking the number of card combinations for each hand divided by the total number of combinations for the range of hands. For example, with AA we have 6 combinations out of a total of 66, which is .09.

[17] For the charts, AK represents both suited and off-suit hands. AKs represents only the suited hands. AKo represents the off-suit hands.

	Combinations	Probability	App. Win % for 88	Totals
AA	6	.07	.195	.014
KK	6	.07	.19	.013
QQ	6	.07	.19	.013
JJ	6	.07	.19	.013
TT	6	.07	.18	.013
AK	16	.195	.54	.107
AQ	16	.195	.55	.106
AJ	16	.195	.55	.106
KQs	4	.05	.51	.026
Total	82			.41 or 41%

Of course, calculating all of this in your head is not that easy. But we can learn common scenarios and work them out beforehand. For example, how often does Ax win against a standard raiser? How often will a small pocket pair win against a standard raiser? How often will two small cards win against a standard raiser? How often does a combination of one high card and one small card like K8 win against a standard raiser? Once you learn the probabilities for the most common situations, you can make general approximations that will help you with your decisions.

The following scenario will give you a start in creating basic generalizations that can be used as guidelines to help with the decision-making process. It takes a common scenario and looks at how several different types of hands stack up against a set range of hands.

You are in the final 15 of a multi-table tournament and are already in the money. The blinds are $1000-$2000 with $200 antes. You are short-stacked with only $4000 in chips remaining after having just paid the big blind. A player from early position with an average stack raises to $6000. There is $11,000 in the pot and you are faced with a $4,000 call from the big blind. The pot is offering 2.75 to 1 pot odds. The raiser is relatively tight and you decide that he would raise with the following hands: AA, KK, QQ, JJ, TT, AK, and AQs. What do you do when holding ATo? 66? 54o? K8s?

ATo vs. the early position raiser
Again, we will use the same type of chart to determine an approximate winning percentage. Realize that the number of combinations for your opponent will vary some since you already have an ace in your hand. This reduces the possibility that your opponent is holding an ace:

	Combinations	Probability	App. Win % for ATo	Totals
AA	3	.07	.08	.006
KK	6	.14	.29	.04
QQ	6	.14	.29	.04
JJ	6	.14	.29	.04
TT	6	.14	.31	.04
AK	12	.29	.26	.073
AQs	3	.07	.25	.018
Total	42			.26 or 26%

.26 is 2.85 to 1 against improving and you have 2.75 to 1 pot odds. This is basically a break-even decision, although just slightly on the negative side from an expectation perspective. Given your short stack and the fact that you will have to pay the small blind on the next hand, this is a good situation to try and get back into the tournament to give yourself a chance at coming back to win. I would "gamble" with this break-even bet given the typical payout structures of tournaments. If this were a cash game, your decision would not really matter either way since it is basically a break-even decision.

(any) lesser pair   2 to 1

66 vs. the early position raiser

	Combinations	Probability	App. Win % for 66	Totals
AA	6	.12	.20	.024
KK	6	.12	.20	.024
QQ	6	.12	.19	.023
JJ	6	.12	.19	.023
TT	6	.12	.19	.023
AK	16	.32	.54	.173
AQs	4	.08	.52	.042
Total	50			.33 or 33%

.33 is 2 to 1 against improving and you are getting 2.75 to 1 pot odds. This gives you an easy decision and you should call.

54o vs. the early position raiser

	Combinations	Probability	App. Win % for 54	Totals
AA	6	.12	.17	.02
KK	6	.12	.19	.023
QQ	6	.12	.19	.023
JJ	6	.12	.19	.023
TT	6	.12	.18	.022
AK	16	.32	.37	.118
AQs	4	.08	.36	.029
Total	50			.26 or 26%

on pg 105 he said .26 = 2.85 to 1 ?

.26 is 2.9 to 1 against improving and you are only getting 2.75 to 1 pot odds. Looking at the calculations you have a negative expectation. Sometimes in tournaments we still might take some gambles depending on the stack sizes, blinds, quality of opponents, and payout structure. For example, if the remaining field included the top pros in the world, it might be wise to gamble a little with a hand that has a slightly negative expectation. Realize that in the particular situation we have described, you will have very little left should you fold. Your stack will not be large enough to get the big blind to fold a hand. This still might be a situation for a gamble even though the odds do not quite justify it. If this was a cash game you should fold, as you must simply go by the mathematical expectation.

K8s vs. the early position raiser

	Combinations	Probability	App. Win % for K8s	Totals
AA	6	.14	.16	.022
KK	3	.07	.12	.008
QQ	6	.14	.31	.044
JJ	6	.14	.31	.044
TT	6	.14	.31	.044
AK	12	.28	.28	.079
AQs	4	.09	.36	.033
Total	43			.27 or 27%

.27 is 2.7 to 1 against improving and you are getting 2.75 to 1 pot odds. This is pretty much the same situation as AT and 54 and is close to a break-even decision, although slightly profitable.

✳

Reviewing these scenarios, we see that ATo, 54o, and K8s were all very close to having an expectation close to 0. These hands basically are even in strength when going to a showdown against this particular range of hands! I expect that this will surprise many of you. Sometimes in Hold'em we know we are behind but can still justify a call before the flop given the pot odds and our short stack. Many people do not think of pre-flop play as a drawing situation but these occur all the time in tournaments when you have to make a play with a borderline hand hoping to double up. This leads us into the next section, which puts us in similar situations but, for whatever reason, you are unable to put your opponent on a specific range of hands.

Facing Random Hands Before the Flop

At times you will be faced with all-in decisions before the flop where you are up against a random hand. This generally occurs in tournaments when either you or your opponent is short-stacked but will also occasionally occur in a cash game. Whether or not you are drawing depends on your cards but this is a good spot to discuss these types of situations. It is important to realize that sometimes you ought to call even though you might have a junk hand. All of this discussion focuses on situations where you are fairly certain that you will be heads-up.

The charts on pages 226-237 can help with these types of decisions. For example, you are in the small blind and everyone folds to you. Either you or the big blind has a very small stack. You look down to find J♠ 6♠. Looking at the charts we see that J♠ 6♠ wins a tad more than half the time (50.6%) against a random hand. You can now determine whether or not to go all-in against a random hand from the big blind based on how much is in the pot and how much is remaining in your stack and his stack. Note that we are discussing situations where either you or your opponent has a small stack. Obviously you would not go all-in here when you both have large stacks, as you would be risking too much in relation to the blinds if your opponent has a monster hand.

50.6% is basically a coin flip. However, there is already dead money in the pot with the blinds. If the pot also contains antes, there is even more dead money. If you know your opponent will call with any hand given the size of each of your stacks, you can move all-in with the knowledge that you are in a coin flip situation while there is already dead money in the pot. The same idea works if an aggressive opponent puts you all-in when you are in the big blind. If you know that your opponent would raise with anything, you can use the random hand charts to help with your decisions.

The following hand examples look at some common scenarios and how you can use odds to make good decisions.

No-Limit Tournament. You are in the middle of a tournament with only $600 left in chips after posting the big blind. The blinds are $300-$600. It is folded to an aggressive player in the small blind with a large stack. He puts you all-in. You look down to find 8♥ 4♣. What should you do?

The first thing to realize is that your opponent would probably raise with any hand hoping to knock you out of the tournament. He is getting decent odds to do so. He only has to risk $900 to win $1500 should you call. Those odds make a raise a good play with almost every hand. However, you are a little smarter than that and will not just back away with a bad hand. Although 8♥ 4♣ is junk, it will still win about 39.5% of the time against a random hand. You are being offered 1.5 to 1, which is not a disaster. Now look at the pot odds. You have $600 left to call with the chance of winning $1800. You are getting 3 to 1 pot odds. With those kind of pot odds, you do not even need to look at your cards to make a decision. It is a no-brainer and you can call with even 32o. You are basically *pot-committed* in this situation after posting the big blind.

No-Limit Tournament. You are late in a tournament with $600-$1200 blinds and are one of the chip leaders. The small blind is a conservative player with an average stack and is fighting to make the money. The big blind only has $1000 in chips remaining after posting the big blind. You are on the button and everyone folds to you. You look down to see KTo. What do you do?

KTo is not exactly a powerhouse in No-Limit Hold'em. However, the big blind is short-stacked so he cannot hurt you. He will be forced to call all-in given the pot odds he will be receiving. Your hand is a 60% favorite to win against a single random hand. If the small blind folds, you are risking $2200 to win $2800, which is 1.3 to 1 pot odds. You are getting decent pot odds on a hand that is a favorite to win. However, you need to worry a little about the small blind. There is always the possibility that he wakes up with a monster hand and puts you all-in forcing you to fold. On the other hand, this player is quite conservative and is fighting to make the money. He probably will not make a move unless he has a monster. He would probably fold hands like AJ, KQ, 77, and maybe even AQ. You finally decide that he is quite conservative and will not risk his stack unless he has a hand that is equivalent to a raising hand in early position from my starting hand charts provided in the Appendix. Referencing the charts we see that these hands are only dealt 4% of the time.

You can now determine your exact expectation for raising with this hand. 96% of the time you get to battle the big blind and 4% of the time you are forced into folding by the small blind. Assume you raise to $3000. Your expectation is as follows: .96[.60(2800) - .40(2200)] + .04 [-3000] = $648. With a positive expectation you decide to raise.

Looking at this formula in layman terms we get the following:
- ♣ 96% of the time you face the big blind.
- ♦ 60% of the time against the big blind you win the $2800 that will be in the pot against his random hand.
- ♥ 40% of the time against the big blind you will lose the $2200 you have invested.
- ♠ 4% of the time the small blind will go all-in and you will be forced to fold, losing your $3000 bet.

Semi-Bluffing Before the Flop

So far our discussion has focused on evaluating the probability of winning versus a random hand in an all-in situation. The possibility that your opponent might fold was not considered since we were looking at situations where either you or your opponent is pot-committed.

This section focuses on a strategy that is essential to aggressive No-Limit tournament play. Stealing blinds and antes is critical to your survival in tournaments. This becomes more crucial as your stack size diminishes in relation to the blinds and antes that you must pay each round.

Key Concept: There are many pre-flop situations where you decide to either move all-in or put your opponent all-in based on the combination of the probability that your opponent will fold and the probability that your hand would win if he calls.

Similar to situations where we make semi-bluffs after the flop, sometimes you might semi-bluff before the flop hoping for a fold while at the same time realizing you still have a chance to improve to the best hand should your opponent call.

For example, suppose you are in the small blind with a weak holding like 9♠ 3♣. For reference, the blinds are $1,000-$2,000 and the big blind has $8,000. You have a large stack and decide to put your opponent all-in. By putting your opponent all-in, you are hoping to win the pot immediately. Your raise might get your opponent to fold a hand like Kx, Qx, or Jx. However, if your opponent calls, you still have a chance to win the pot by hitting a good hand. Your raise becomes profitable when you consider the combination of the probability that your opponent will fold[18] along with the probability that your hand will win in a showdown. Sometimes it is profitable to raise an opponent with any hand if there is a decent probability that he will fold.

---

[18] This scenario assumes a relatively tight opponent. Some opponents might call in this situation with any hand while others might play very conservatively.

I played an interesting hand in New Zealand a few years ago trying to apply this concept. I had a big stack and it was folded to me in the small blind. I looked down at 52o and decided to put my opponent all-in. 52o has only a 34% chance of winning against a random hand but I evaluated this hand a little further. His stack was quite small but large enough that I thought he would fold unless he had a decent hand. Given this reasoning, I thought the probability was quite high that he would fold and I still had the possibility of winning even if he called.

Calculating the expectation of this play is straightforward. Assume an 80% chance that my opponent would fold to a raise. I do not remember the exact blind structure at the time but we can make up some numbers just for the example's sake. We will assume the blinds were $100-$200 and my opponent had $800 left in chips while I had $5000. We have already determined that he would not play just any random hand so our winning percentage will be less that 34%. For the purpose of this example we will assume you will win 30% of the time should he call. Therefore, the expectation is $.8 \times 300 + .2[.3(1100) - .7(1000)] = \$166$.

My opponent called and to my surprise turned over 42o! I never thought I would be in a dominating position with a hand like 52 off-suit! Unfortunately, we ended up splitting the pot[19].

What was my opponent's expectation of calling in this situation? Since I raised, he must assume that I have at least two over-cards and possibly a pocket pair. But let us assume he just thinks I will raise with any random hand. In this case, 42 will win 33% of the time against a random hand. Therefore, his expectation by calling is $.33 (1300) - .67 (800) = -107$. His expectation is worse assuming I would not raise with trash hands. In this situation my opponent did not recognize that he was not getting correct pot odds to play against any two cards. However, I also made a mistake in this hand. I did not recognize that my opponent did not quite understand pot odds and would call with any hand. If I had known he would call with any hand I would have folded with such a weak hand.

---

[19] Actually, there was an 18% chance that we would split the pot.

Generally, when one player makes a mistake the other one benefits. In this case, we both made mistakes on the same hand! It is not mathematically correct for my opponent to call even if he knows I will raise with any random hand. His hand is too weak given the size of the raise. On the other hand, my hand was too weak to play against an opponent who would call with any hand. The expectation in this case is calculated as follows: .34(1100) - .66(1000) = -$286.

Sometimes good players make the mistake of thinking their opponents will make the correct play. A common error is trying to bet an opponent out of a pot when you think he is weak but you are playing an opponent who rarely folds a hand. It is crucial to understand what plays will work against each specific opponent and what play will not. This hand is a perfect example. It ends up that my opponent made a play with an expectation of -107 and I made a play with an expectation of -286. Sometimes we are not as smart as we think we are.

All-in on the Flop

In the chapter on applying odds in Limit Hold'em, we looked at how you can calculate odds with two cards to come and showed a chart that summarized the odds. This chart is extremely helpful in making all-in decisions on the flop in No-Limit Hold'em. When an opponent bets an amount that puts either of you all-in and you hold a strong draw, the first question that arises is, "Do you have the right pot odds to justify calling in this situation?" Since one of you is all-in, there are no implied pot odds to consider. This situation also occurs when the bet may not be all-in but is effectively all-in if either you or your opponent is pot-committed to call any additional bets.

These situations are basically straightforward. As we learned in the section on drawing in Limit, simply determine your outs, discount them, and then compare the odds against improving with two cards to come versus the pot odds[20].

The following examples demonstrate drawing decisions on the flop in a No-Limit Hold'em game.

No-Limit Tournament. The blinds are $200-$400 and you are on the button with T♠ 9♠. The average stack is $5000. An early player limps and you call. The small blind folds and the flop comes K♠ 5♣ 2♠. The early player moves all-in for $3600. You have $4000 left in chips. Should you call?

First determine your pot odds. There was $1400 in the pot before the flop and your opponent bets $3600. You have to risk $3600 to win $5000 giving you pot odds of 1.4 to 1, (1400 + 3600)/3600). Assuming your opponent has at least a pair of kings, you have nine outs to improve

---

[20] Sometimes there are situations in tournaments where you would intentionally make a play that has a negative expectation. Conversely, sometimes you pass up on positive expectations. Examples include taking gambles when you are low-stacked and playing conservatively when you are on the bubble. In a tournament, you might also pass up on a draw that is a slight favorite when there is plenty of time to find better opportunities. The focus of this book is how to apply odds so we are focusing on calculating expectations. Just understand that expectation is not always the only criteria you use when making poker decisions.

to a flush. You also have a backdoor-straight draw, which adds a little to your outs. Your opponent could have a draw to a full-house which requires a slight discount on your outs. Another consideration is that the big blind might also be sitting on a bigger draw. In that case, you could have outs to your T or 9. If you assume these small considerations cancel each other out, you can calculate the odds based on nine outs. Using our charts for two cards to come, we see that 9 outs have a 1.9 to 1 chance of improving. You are only getting 1.4 to 1 pot odds so you should fold.

$5-10 No-Limit Cash Game. You have just bought in for $500 and limp in with A♦ Q♦. Two opponents call and the button raises to $50. You decide to call, as do the other two opponents. Four players see the flop of J♦ T♦ 5♣. You bet out $150. The next two players fold and the button puts you all-in. What should you do?

You have $300 left and there is $815 in the pot giving you 2.7 to 1 pot odds. You have nine outs to the nut flush and three more outs to the nut straight. However, in case your opponent holds a set, you need to discount your outs slightly for the possibility that you could still hit a flush or straight only to lose to a full-house. You also have over-cards that might possibly be good if you are against a hand like KK or AJ. I would estimate about 12 douts. 12 douts is 1.2 to 1 against improving and you are getting 2.7 to 1 pot odds making this an easy call.

All-in on the Turn

You follow the same process here as you would on the flop except that you only have one card left which can improve your hand. At this point there are 46 cards left in the deck so just divide the number of douts you have by 46 to get the probability of improving. The odds against improving are simply (46-x)/x with "x" equaling the number of douts.

All-in decisions on the turn are straightforward. However, it is not too common to call an all-in bet on the turn with a draw in No-Limit.

Key Concept: Realize that most draws are big underdogs with only one card left to come. The only time you might find yourself calling an all-in bet on the turn when drawing is when either you or your opponent have a small stack and you can therefore justify the odds of calling.

But in most situations, your opponent will bet an amount that is too high for you to call given the small chance of improving your hand with only one card to come.

Effective Implied Pot Odds

So far we have looked at situations that put either you or your opponent all-in. These types of decisions occur more frequently in the later stages of a tournament, as the blinds are high in relation to everyone's stack size.

During the early stages of a tournament you will often be faced with decisions that do not put you all-in. In these cases, implied pot odds become an important factor in your decisions. The bigger the stacks are in comparison to the bets, the bigger role implied pot odds have in a decision.

Many people like to throw around the term "implied pot odds". The problem is that there is sometimes confusion with the definition. Implied pot odds should include the amount of bets you *expect* to win from your opponent. Some say, or at least act in such a way, that implied pot odds include the amount of bets you *could* win from your opponent. Expectation and potential are two very different things. To clarify and to ensure you have the correct mindset when making strategic decisions, a much better term to use in your poker vocabulary is *effective implied pot odds*.

The effective implied pot odds is simply the relationship between the amount in the pot and the amount that you *expect* to win from your opponent(s) should you hit your hand compared to the bets required to play the hand. This is similar to the definition of implied pot odds but "effective" ensures that you are considering the amount you expect to win, and not the potential. Drawing to a long shot, betting, and then watching your opponent fold does not have a positive expectation if you based your decision on the expectation that you would win your opponent's entire stack.

For example, in the early rounds of the World Series of Poker main event, you start out with $10,000 in chips and $25-$50 blinds. If you face a $100 bet on the flop, you have the potential of winning $10,000 which would give you 100 to 1 implied pot odds. If you face a $1000 bet, these implied pot odds are now 10 to 1. Many players make the mistake of making decisions based on the potential win rather than the average win they expect to make in the long-term. The potential win is part of the equation but you cannot make decisions expecting this to happen all the time.

Determining the effective implied pot odds in Limit Hold'em is much easier than it is in No-Limit Hold'em. Most of the time in Limit Hold'em you can expect to win an additional 1-5 big bets after the flop depending on the number of opponents in the hand and the strength of their hands.

In No-Limit the effective implied pot odds are not so clear. For example, even though a bet of $100 might represent 100 to 1 potential implied pot odds given your stack sizes, the effective implied pot odds are probably much less. Your opponents will often back down on the turn in No-Limit. On the other hand, if he has top set you will most likely win a large portion, if not all, of his stack. Your decision should be based on the average expectation given all of the different scenarios that could play out given the range of hands you put your opponent on.

Key Concept: Determining your effective implied pot odds in No-Limit is dependant on the type of opponent you are up against and the range of hands you put him on.

The effective implied pot odds in No-Limit have a big impact on strategy when comparing No-Limit to Limit. In Limit Hold'em, you need a large pot to justify drawing to a gut-shot straight. In No-Limit, the pot does not need to be very large at the moment if you think there is a good chance you will get paid off handsomely should you hit your hand. This same concept can be applied to starting hand strategy. Some players will play many hands in hopes of hitting a big hand since the implied pot odds are so great. On the other hand, you might not get paid off at all.

For example, with a flop of 9♣ 6♥ 4♦, you will not have very good effective implied pot odds if your opponent is sitting on a hand like A♣ Q♦ or even a hand like 8♥ 8♣. Even if your opponent has a large stack, your opponent won't give you very much action so your effective implied pot odds will not be very high. If your opponent has an over-pair, you will likely get some action but it still may be difficult to get his whole stack early in a tournament depending on the opponent and the situation.

Determining your effective implied pot odds takes experience and a good understanding of your opponents. Weak opponents tend to play their hands too strongly. Players like these are willing to play over-pairs very strongly without worrying about sets. They will push top pairs with a weak kicker. Your effective implied pot odds are much higher against opponents like these than stronger opponents since you have a better chance of winning their entire stack if they have a decent hand.

A good example of this occurred at the 2004 World Series of Poker. We were in the 2nd level and a weak player from middle position made a standard size raise. The next opponent called and I raised from the big blind with QQ. Both opponents called and the flop came out KQx. I bet a small amount and the next opponent made a significant size raise. At this point, the pot was quite large so I just decided to move all-in. My opponent called and turned over AK. Even though this is not a drawing hand, it demonstrates how some players are willing to risk all of their chips with just mediocre hands. I'm not sure what this opponent thought he could beat given all the strength I had shown up to that point but he is the kind of opponent I wish I had at my table all the time. Against these types of opponents you will often have very high effective implied pot odds.

Key Concept: Your effective implied pot odds are generally higher against weaker opponents than they are against strong opponents.

Strong opponents are always playing a game of survival. They might be willing to take a stab at the pot on a bluff or attempt to protect a strong hand but they will bail out if it appears that it is likely that they are up against a very strong hand. They will sometimes bet in a fashion where they hope to lose the minimum if their opponent has a super strong hand. Against these types of opponents your effective implied pot odds will be less than they are against amateur players who will sometimes get married to their hand.

One skill that separates expert players from the amateur player is that expert players do a better job at determining their effective implied pot odds in each particular situation. Occasionally you will see an expert player make a call on a draw that on the surface seems crazy, but in reality, they were probably assessing their opponent and the situation and determined that their was a high likelihood of winning their opponent's entire stack if they hit their hand. In the same situation against a strong opponent they are likely to fold their hand.

When you face a tough call on a draw, always think of your effective implied pot odds. Do not get trapped in looking at your opponent's entire stack, but rather, concentrate on figuring out how much of your opponent's stack you think you could win on average if you hit your hand. It is not always what you could win, but rather, what you expect to win.

The following examples look at how effective implied pot odds are used to make drawing decisions.

No-Limit $10-$20 Cash Game. The cutoff raises to $35 and you decide to call on the button with Q♥ T♣. Both of the blinds fold and the flop comes J83 rainbow. You both have about $2,000 in chips and your opponent bets $100 into a $100 pot. Do the effective implied pot odds justify a call?

First realize that we cannot answer this question without an understanding of your opponent. We know you are 10.5 to 1 to hit your straight. This does not offer a favorable situation given that your pot odds are 2 to 1. However, you do have 20 to 1 implied pot odds if you are able to get your opponent to commit his stack should you hit your draw. The question becomes whether or not you can win enough from your opponent if you hit your hand. You need to be able to make at least an additional $850 to justify the odds against hitting your straight. Against a weak opponent, there is a decent chance you can do this if your opponent has top pair or better. Realize however that your opponent might not be holding very much at all. Against a strong opponent, it is unlikely you will make a lot of money off this hand unless he has a big pocket pair or top pair, and even then, you are not guaranteed of getting a big payoff. This is an easy fold against a strong opponent and a borderline call against a weak opponent.

No-Limit Major Tournament. Early in a tournament you are in the cutoff with A♣ 3♣ and call a raise of $200 from an early position player. The flop comes K♥ 4♦ 2♠ and the raiser bets $400. You both hold about $10,000 in chips. The raiser is wearing a shirt from an online poker site, which seems to indicate that he won his entry through an online satellite. He also appears a little nervous. What do you do?

It can sometimes be dangerous to generalize, but in this case, there is not too much downside in thinking that online players are known for their willingness to risk their stacks with top pair. You have to risk $400 for the possibility of hitting a monster straight on the turn. If your opponent holds AA, KK, or AK, you have a good chance of raking in a very nice pot and possibly your opponent's entire stack. Even if you miss your draw, you still might be able to steal the pot on the turn if your opponent indicates weakness while holding something like QQ or JJ. 10,000/400 represents implied pot odds of 25 to 1. Your effective implied pot odds are probably somewhere close to that if your opponent has hit this flop. This is a good hand to call and try to hit a big pot.

2004 World Series of Poker Main Event: No-Limit. This next hand is an interesting hand I played during the 2004 World Series of Poker main event. It demonstrates a mistake I made before the flop by not considering the implied pot odds I was giving my opponent.

It was late afternoon on the first day of the 2004 World Series of Poker main event. The blinds were $100-$200. Andy Bloch, a well-known pro, had about $30,000 in chips and raised under-the-gun to $600. $30,000 in chips was a very good amount at this stage in the tournament. I had not played with Andy before but my impressions were that he was a straightforward solid conservative player. I was sitting in the cutoff and looked down at A♥ Q♥. I also had about $30K in chips. I was not too excited about playing a flop with this hand against Andy when he had raised under-the-gun. My first instinct was that Andy would not want to battle with another big stack unless he had a monster hand. In this case, if I re-raised, Andy would either re-raise with a monster or fold. I re-raised hoping to pick up the pot. To my surprise, Andy called and we saw a flop.

The flop came K♦ T♥ 6♥. I had a flush draw and gut-shot straight draw. Andy checked. I decided to check and take the free card hoping to hit my draw. I did not want to risk a check-raise on that type of flop with my big draw. The turn was the 7♣ and Andy bet out $2500.

At this point I was focusing on AK as the most likely hand for Andy. I knew he was a solid conservative player. I did not think he would call a large reraise before the flop against a large stack unless he had a premium hand and AK was a likely candidate. One of the worst mistakes you can make in No-Limit Hold'em is to put yourself in a position where you would have to fold a big draw. If I raised the turn I would be risking that Andy raises me out of the pot.

However, my check on the flop must have looked somewhat suspicious to Andy. I made a big re-raise pre-flop and then came out checking the flop? It very well could look to Andy like I had KK. I decided to raise to $7500 and represent a set of kings hoping to get Andy to fold his AK. I risked losing out on a big draw if Andy came over the top of me but he had to be worried that I had KK...unless he had KK also. KK seemed doubtful though given the pre-flop action.

After a considerable amount of reflection, Andy finally decided to call. I did not expect that! What could he have? He must not believe I have AK beat! What am I going to do now? Fortunately I was left with a very easy decision. The river was a heart giving me the nut flush. I decided to bet enough to get a big call from Andy without breaking him. Andy showed TT and I walked away with a huge pot. My check on the flop paid huge dividends, as he indeed must have been worried about KK.

This is an interesting hand from many different perspectives. One of the main lessons in this hand is how implied pot odds impact a hand. During my thinking process, I thought I could raise Andy out of the pot before the flop unless he had a monster. What I failed to realize is that since I had a big stack also, Andy had great implied pot odds for drawing to a set with any pair. Given the size of my stack, he probably suspected that I had a large pair and he felt he could possibly win my whole stack if he managed to hit a set. Fortunately, my mistake paid off on this hand as I was able to hit a huge draw. This pre-flop mistake, however, put me in a position where I had to make some very tough and risky decisions after the flop.

Another interesting point about this hand was how I evaluated Andy. I knew he was a straightforward, solid, conservative player. Given this, I was able to make my raise on the turn, as I was confident Andy would be worried about a set of kings. If I was against an unknown or weak opponent, I probably would not have made this play, as I cannot expect all players to lay down a hand like AK. It turns out Andy did have a monster but he was still worried that I had an even bigger hand. Fortunately for me, he decided not to risk that I had a better hand, which gave me the chance to hit a huge hand.

A summary of the main points of this section is as follows:

♠ In No-Limit, the implied pot odds can sometimes allow you to take speculative draws even when the pot is not very large.

♣ It is important to evaluate the *effective* implied pot odds against a particular opponent. Some opponents are more likely to bet away their chips than others so you can never assume that you will always take your opponent's stack when you hit a big draw.

♦ In No-Limit, always be aware of the implied pot odds you are receiving as well as the implied pot odds you are giving your opponent.

Protecting Your Hand

Once you decide that you are going to take the initiative with a No-Limit hand, the next decision is determining how much you are going to bet. The amount of your bet is always very important. If you bet too little with a good hand, you could be inviting your opponent to hit a long shot, which might cost you your entire stack. If you bet too much, you might find yourself in a situation where you are only winning small pots and losing large pots. A key part of the decision in determining how much to bet is dependent on the pot odds and implied pot odds.

This discussion is only going to look at how odds and probabilities play a factor in protecting your hand. Realize that other factors, such as psychological warfare, are important in No-Limit. Sometimes we might make a small bet with a big hand hoping that our opponents would sense a bluff and try to make a play at us. At other times, we might bet big trying to indicate a bluff. Both are two ways of using psychology during a hand.

A good example of this comes from Day 5 of the 2004 World Series of Poker main event. I was dealt AA under-the-gun and intentionally put in a larger than normal raise. I had been at this new table for about an hour and had played very few hands. I was getting dealt trash hands and was still trying to feel out the other players. After an hour of being quite inactive, I was dealt AA. How could I get any action after being so tight for an hour? Given the tight image I had developed, most players would probably run for the hills if I made only the standard raise. By over-betting, I was hoping that my opponents would sense that I did not want action and make a play at me. It turns out that Al Krux obliged me by deciding to move all-in with TT. I happily called only to see my dreams start to fade away when a T fell on the river. Ten minutes later, I was knocked out in 33rd place. My strategy worked, but I did not end up with the result for which I had hoped.

There are many psychological aspects that play a part in the strategies you might use in No-Limit. This psychological aspect is not the focus of this book. This book focuses specifically on how odds and probabilities can be used to make good poker decisions. The first step is learning the mathematical foundation of poker including how much you ought to bet. Once you master the foundation, you can then learn more advanced plays in terms of the psychology to use against each individual opponent.

Determining How Much to Bet
The amount you bet on the flop is a critical decision in No-Limit Hold'em. Look at this extreme example just to demonstrate a point. You are heads-up in a major poker championship and are dealt JJ. The blinds are $10,000-$20,000 and you raise to $75,000 pre-flop. A very tricky, loose opponent calls. There is now $150,000 in the pot. The flop comes J73 rainbow and your opponent checks. You both have about $880,000 remaining in chips. How much should you bet?

Of course there are always many factors that should impact your betting in No-Limit but we are going to look at one of the most critical factors - protecting your hand. You have flopped top set and the board is relatively harmless. Assume you decide to slow-play and bet $40,000. Your opponent calls and the turn card is an 8. Then, in a flurry, you are both all-in. You turn over your set only to look in exasperation as your opponent turns over T9 for a straight.

Your opponent was only getting 5 to 1 pot odds to call on the flop on a draw that was 10.5 to 1; however, implied pot odds are critical in No-Limit as you can sometimes break your opponent or vice versa. In this case, your opponent was getting good implied pot odds when he only had to call a bet of $40,000 in hopes of hitting his miracle 8. With 10.5 to1 odds against hitting the straight, he must feel like he can win $420K to justify calling. There is already $190K in the pot so he must be able to extract $230K more from your stack to justify calling. In this case, if you have a big over-pair there is a good chance that he can take your whole stack if he hits a huge hand. By betting too little, you put your opponent into a position where he was correct to call.

Key Concept: Protecting your hand is crucial to your survival in No-Limit tournaments, especially when there is the possibility that you could lose your whole stack.

Many players ask, "How can I protect my entire stack when it is so big compared to the size of the pot?" Focus on betting an amount that will protect the total amount you are willing to commit to the pot. In essence, you are protecting against your opponent's effective implied pot odds. For example, sometimes your opponent might call a bet, hit a draw, and you would fold. In this case, you are not giving your opponent implied pot odds since you are not committing more money to the pot.

Key Concept: Try to bet amounts which will put your opponents into situations where they will make mistakes by calling.

There are four steps to take when determining how much to bet in order to provide protection for your hand:
1. Determine potential dangers with the flop versus your hand.
2. Identify the amount you want to protect. This includes the money already in the pot and the amount of money you are willing to commit to the pot.
3. Calculate the break-even bet amount. Divide the amount you want to protect by the odds against your opponent of improving to the winning hand.
4. Based on the break-even amount determined in Step 3, determine how much to bet.

The first step deserves more discussion. You should always be evaluating how the texture of the board impacts the play of the hand. My first book, *Internet Texas Hold'em*, discussed in detail the potential dangers of each type of flop. Are flush draws possible? Could someone have an open-ended straight draw? What about a gut-shot draw? Could my opponent have 5 outs to two pair or trips? Maybe it is likely that my opponent only has 3 outs in a scenario where we both hold top pair (AK vs. KQ with a flop of K82). Each of these dangers must be evaluated. All flops and all hands are not created equal!

To look at these steps in practice, reconsider the previous example where you have $880K left in chips while flopping top set with a board of J73.

Step 1 - Evaluate the flop to identify any dangers. Note that all of the following hands have gut-shot possibilities: T9, T8, 98, 65, 64, and 54. This is actually a decent number of hands that you need to worry about.

Step 2 – Identify the amount you want to protect. If you want to protect your chip stack, you must bet in a manner that protects the amount in your stack with what is already in the pot. With 880K in chips and 150K in the pot, you need to protect $1,030.

Step 3 – Calculate the break-even bet amount. Your opponent could have a gut shot draw, which is 10.5 to 1 against improving. Dividing the amount you want to protect by the odds gives you $98,000 ($1,030K/10.5).

Step 4 -- Determine how much to bet. If you bet slightly more than $98,000, something like $110,000, you ensure that your opponent is not getting the correct odds to call. If your opponent calls he is making a mistake. There is no guarantee that you will win but at least you are forcing your opponent into making a mistake because of the *amount you bet*. Of course, you could also go all-in (which would really discourage callers), but you also want to encourage action, thereby giving yourself a better chance to win a big pot.

If your opponent hits a pair on the flop, such as a hand like 87 with our J73 flop, he might call thinking he has the correct implied pot odds to draw to two pair. If he hits two pair you will now break him. When you protect your hand, you actually want your opponent to call since he is making a mistake in doing so. Note that even if you bet slightly less like $98K, an opponent should not call, as he cannot be sure that he can extract your entire stack. The $98K is simply the mathematical amount that truly protects your hand.

Understand that protecting your hand is not always the only consideration. Sometimes you might be unsure that you have the best hand. For example, you might have an over-pair and your opponent could have a set. In these cases, you have to balance how much you want to protect your hand with the possible risk that your opponent already has a better hand.

Hand Examples

In all of the following hand examples you hold AA. The flop comes T♣ 8♣ 4♦. If your opponent holds a flush draw, he is approximately 4 to 1 to improve on the next card (37/9). To protect against the pot odds, you should bet more than 1/3 of the pot. For example, if there is $3000 in the pot and you bet $1000, your opponent is getting exactly 4 to 1 to call. Once you apply the effective implied pot odds that your opponent has, it is apparent that you should bet more than 1/3 the pot to protect your hand and stack. By betting the pot, you give your opponent 2 to 1 pot odds while he is 4 to 1 against improving his hand. This is generally sufficient; although you must be willing to give up on your hand in some situations should a 3rd card of the same suit come.

The flop comes K♣ 8♠ 2♦. This is an excellent flop for an over-pair. There are no flush or straight possibilities. Your only concerns are sets and two pair. If your opponent has a set, then you are the one needing to improve. An opponent with a pair, where one of his cards matches the board, has five outs, which are approximately 8 to 1 against improving. Therefore, you could bet 1/3 the pot and your opponent would not be getting correct pot odds to call, as you would be giving him 4 to 1 pot odds while he is 8 to 1 against improving.

For example, if there is $4000 in the pot and you bet $1300, your opponent is getting about 4 to 1 pot odds to improve. Based on the pot odds, you are forcing him to make a mistake by calling with a hand like KQ or 98. However, you also need to consider the implied pot odds. If he improves his hand, he will be able to take more money off you on the turn and/or river before you realize that you are beat. To offset this potential loss, you might want to bet 1/2 to 2/3 the size of the pot. For example, if you bet $2000 he is only getting 3 to 1 pot odds to call while he would need to win over $16,000 total to justify the implied pot odds. Therefore, your opponent would need to feel that he could win another $10,000 from you to justify calling for the effective implied odds. If you feel this is a possibility, you might consider betting more than ½ the pot.

Reconsider the above example and let us assume that there is now only $3000 in the pot and you have $21,000 remaining in your stack. Your opponent is a loose aggressive player and is the chip leader. How much do you need to bet to fully protect your hand given a flop of K♣ 8♠ 2♦? Assuming your opponent holds a pair, his best-case scenario would be 8 to 1 against improving (assuming he does not already have you beat). He will be a big favorite to win the $3000 in the pot plus your stack of $21K if he hits[21]. He stands to gain $24K in this scenario should he improve.

A break-even proposition for him would be a call of $3000 since his implied pot odds would now be 8 to 1. Therefore, you need to bet more than the size of the pot to have a positive expectation on your bet. By betting anything less than the size of the pot, you are offering a justified scenario for your opponent to call if you plan to go all-in regardless of the turn card. By betting more than $3000, you force your opponent to make a mistake by calling.

The more you can get him to call, the better your expectation becomes. For example, a bet of $5000 has a positive expectation, but if you can get your opponent to call a bet of $8000 that would obviously be even better. The best way to fully protect your hand would be to go all-in but this would only win you a $3000 pot most of the time. By betting an amount that you hope your opponent will call, you improve your expectation even further, as long as the amount is greater than $3000.

---

[21] There is the possibility that you could improve to the best hand on the river.

The above scenario assumed that you were willing to risk your entire stack on the hand with your over-pair. As we discussed earlier, this is not always wise depending on the stack sizes in relation to the blinds and the type of opponent you are against. Sometimes the correct strategy is to keep the pot small to minimize the effective implied pot odds of your *opponent* should he be sitting on a monster hand. This protects you against being eliminated from the tournament. On the other hand, you risk giving your opponent the correct odds to call if you decide to keep the pot small.

This is the essence of gambling. There are many scenarios in No-Limit Hold'em where you have to make tradeoffs. By betting more than the pot in this particular hand example, you risk putting yourself in a pot-committed situation that could be disastrous if your opponent is sitting on a better hand. These types of decisions separate the experts from the rest of pack. Expert players make better decisions in these types of situations by doing a better job of determining whether their opponent is on a draw or a better hand.

The Standard Size Bet
Most experts recommend betting around ½ the pot to full pot size. How do they come up with this benchmark? Looking at how we use odds and probabilities to protect our hand, we can make some generalizations about how much we ought to bet. The most common scenarios that we face are situations where our opponent might have 4 outs with a gut-shot, 5 outs with a draw to two pair or trips, 8 outs to an open-ended draw, 9 outs to a flush draw, 11 outs to an open-ended straight draw and an over-card, and 12 outs to a flush draw with an over-card.

In normal tournament situations, by making bets that are somewhere between ½ the pot size to full pot, you will be adequately protecting your hand against your opponents hitting their draw while also inviting action from time to time.

Impact of Stack Sizes

As we have discussed, stack sizes are an important factor in No-Limit decisions on whether or not we should draw and how much we should bet. The implied pot odds are the direct result of the size of each player's stack. Determining how much to bet is in direct relation to how much we need to protect. This becomes especially true in tournaments, as you do not have the ability to add to your chips. This topic deserves further attention, as it is the basis for many decisions we make in No-Limit.

The following discussion shows how stack sizes impact your decisions. In each example, the only thing we are changing is the stack sizes of the two players.

The blinds are $15-$30 early in a tournament. An opponent raises to $75 and you look down at 44. You both have about $1,500 in chips. This is a good situation to call as you have the potential of hitting a set and winning a huge pot.

Assume the same situation occurs again but this time your opponent only has $300 in chips rather than $1000. In this case, calling is dubious because the maximum implied pot odds are only about 5.5 to 1 and the odds of hitting your set are 7.5 to 1. The implied pot odds do not justify a call in this situation[22].

What if your opponent has $1000 in chips and you only have $300. This is the same situation as above.

Key Concept: When looking at implied pot odds you only need to consider the amount of the smallest stack between you and your opponent.

Consider another situation. An opponent raises to $70 and you only have $100 left in chips. In this case you will need to make a move soon

---

[22] This example assumes that we do not want to risk a lot of chips with this hand unless we can hit a set. Sometimes there are situations where you can re-raise 44 to get an opponent to fold or you might see a flop and make a big bet against your opponent if the flop is favorable. Realize that re-raising puts you in a situation where at best you are against two overcards and there is the risk that you are against a big pocket pair.

as the blinds are going to eat away at your small stack. This might be a good time to gamble and move all-in. Here we are hoping that we are against just two over-cards and not a big pocket pair. This hand is an example where we take gambles, because of our chip position, which we would normally not want to take.

This is a good place to note that when you are short-stacked in a tournament, it is better to try and raise first-in and all-in while you have *folding equity* rather than be in a situation where you have to call all-in. This gives you the chance of winning the pot uncontested. Of course, you need to do this before your stack gets too small. Once your stack is below 3-4 times the big blind you should expect to be called by any hand since the big blind will be getting good pot odds to call. Of course, you do not always have a choice and you might need to gamble such as in this example with 44.

It should be obvious that you would not move all-in with 44 if both of you had large stacks. In that case, you would either win a small pot or likely be a big underdog in a large pot.

Chip stacks have a big impact on every decision you face. In the examples, the cards were the same but the decision was different as the stack sizes changed in relation to the blinds. In tournaments this type of analysis is critical.

Key Concept: A major part of your decision process concerns evaluating your stack size, the stacks of your opponents, and both of these in relation to the blinds.

I am constantly evaluating each player's stack size during and after every hand. How many chips does the big blind have? How many chips does the raiser have? How many chips does the player acting behind me have? All of these are important considerations when making decisions in No-Limit.

In cash games it is recommended that you re-buy whenever your stack size gets below the maximum buy-in so that you are able to maximize the value of your big hands.

opp. of cash ultra-tight book

It is important to understand how stack sizes impact the style of play during each stage of a tournament. In the early rounds, players will limp a lot more. You will see a lot of flops and players will often be in drawing situations. In the later stages, the blinds are often quite high in relation to each player's stack. In these situations, most hands are decided before the flop so drawing hands decrease considerably in value.

The following discussion looks in more detail at how stack sizes impact decisions both before and after the flop.

Pre-flop Considerations

Throughout our discussion on No-Limit, we have discussed many situations when your stack size impacts your decision. For example, the effective implied pot odds you have before the flop might impact whether or not you even play a hand. The stack size of your opponent might be the difference between calling, folding, raising, or going all-in with a hand like 88. The correct play depends on whether or not you are getting the correct implied pot odds to see a flop. One important consideration that deserves attention is determining when you are pot-committed.

When are you Pot-Committed?

In a tournament, your stack size will often force you into situations that you would normally rather avoid. Generally, once you decide to commit over 1/3 of your stack to a pot before the flop, you must seriously consider being committed to going all-in for a showdown. At 1/2 your stack the decision is a no-brainer except in very rare circumstances. A rare circumstance where you might fold a weak holding is when there is a raise and re-raise by two different opponents.

For example, the blinds are $1500-$3000 with $300 antes and you hold $18,000 in chips. You look down to see AJ in the cutoff. If you raise to $9000, you are pot-committed. Even if the most conservative of players puts you all-in you will be forced to call knowing that you have the worst hand going in. With a pot of at least $31,500, the pot odds are just too good at this point and a call is justified. In this example, your pot odds are at least 3.5 to 1. AJ is getting correct pot odds to call against any hand with the exception of AA. AJ has about a 27% chance of beating AK or AQ, which is just 2.7 to 1, and the pot odds are offering 3.5 to 1.

Once you have committed about 1/3 of your stack to the pot you have a more difficult decision. At this point, your decision should be based on several factors including the type of opponent you are up against. In these cases, make the best estimate of your hand winning against the probable range of your opponent's hand and compare them to the pot odds. Sometimes you can fold and still have enough to get back in the tournament while in other cases you need to risk going all-in for the chance to add to your stack.

Realize that you are never worse than a 3 to 1 underdog unless you are up against an over-pair and that you are frequently closer to only being a 2 to 1 underdog. For example, AJ versus AK is 2.7 to 1, AT versus KK is 2.3 to 1, and 74 versus AK is 1.8 to 1. The situation is generally not as bad as you might think which is why you should often call in situations where you are short-stacked and have committed a large percentage of your stack.

Post-Flop Considerations
We have also discussed many situations where stack sizes impact your decision after the flop. These include situations where you might be facing an all-in bet. These types of situations generally occur when either you or your opponent have a short stack. We also discussed how implied pot odds have a role when there are a lot of chips still in play between you and your opponent. Everything we have discussed in the entire No-Limit section has centered on the stack sizes of the players involved. Be sure to always be aware of the stack sizes of your opponents.

Do they need to make a move soon with even a weak holding? Are they pot-committed? Will the blinds call with any hand given their pot odds? All of these questions should be constantly going through your mind so that you can make the best decisions.

Chapter Review

❑ The main difference between drawing in No-Limit compared to Limit is that implied odds become a much more important factor.

❑ In all-in situations before the flop, determine the probability of winning versus a range of hands that you put your opponent on in the given situation. You can then compare your odds against winning to the pot odds you are receiving to make the correct decision.

❑ When you have a short stack in a tournament, you can often justify calling with weak hands from the blinds based on the good pot odds you are receiving.

❑ Semi-bluffing before the flop with a weak hand can sometimes be profitable against an opponent with a small stack. By raising your opponent all-in, the play can be profitable when you consider the combination of the probability that your opponent will fold along with the probability that your hand will win in a showdown.

❑ Realize that most draws are big underdogs with only one card left to come. The only time you might find yourself calling an all-in bet on the turn when drawing is when either you or your opponent have a small stack and you can therefore justify the odds of calling.

❑ The bigger the stacks are in comparison to the blinds, the bigger role implied pot odds have in a decision.

❑ The effective implied pot odds include the amount that you expect to win from your opponent should you hit your hand. Drawing to a long shot, betting, and then watching your opponent fold does not have a positive expectation if you based your decision on the expectation that you would have implied pot odds.

❑ The effective implied pot odds are generally higher against weaker opponents than they are against strong opponents.

❑ Determining your effective implied pot odds in No-Limit is very dependant on the type of opponent you are up against and the range of hands you put him on.

❑ Protecting your hand is crucial to your survival in No-Limit tournaments, especially when there is the possibility that you could lose your whole stack.

❑ Try to bet amounts which will put your opponents into situations where they will make mistakes by calling.

❑ Protecting your hand does not always mean protecting your entire stack. The amount you should protect is the amount you are willing to commit to the pot. This represents the effective implied pot odds you are giving to your opponent.

❑ In normal tournament situations, by making bets which are somewhere between ½ the pot size to full pot, you will be adequately protecting your hand against your opponents hitting their draw while also inviting action from time to time.

❑ The implied pot odds are the direct result of the size of each player's stack.

❑ When looking at implied pot odds you only need to consider the amount of the smallest stack between you and your opponent.

❑ A major part of your decision process concerns evaluating your stack size, the stack of your opponents, and both of these in relation to the blinds.

❑ In the early and middle stages of No-Limit tournaments, strategy is often focused on implied pot odds giving drawing hands added value. In the later stages of a tournament, players are frequently forced into all-in situations before the flop when the blinds represent a high percentage of their stack.

Test Your Skills

The hands to "test your skills" are broken down into two sections: cash games and tournaments. The concepts are similar in both so I recommend going through both sets of hands even though you might not play both types of games.

Cash Games

$1-$2 Blinds: No-Limit Cash Game.

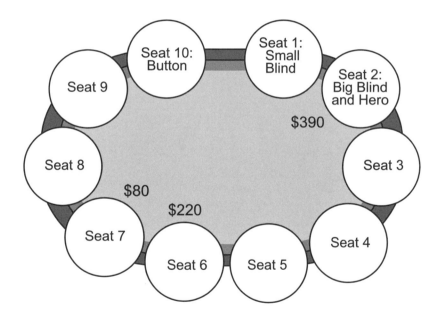

An early player raises to $4. Two middle players and the button all call. You call with 6♣ 5♣ from the big blind. Five players see the flop of Q♠ 4♦ 3♣. Seat 6 bets $6 and seat 7 raises to $25. There is $52 in the pot. What do you do?

Answer: Your open-ended straight draw is almost 5 to 1 against improving on the next card (39/8). You are only getting 2 to 1 pot odds and there is a chance that the original bettor could re-raise. This is an easy decision. Fold.

In the actual hand everyone folded.

$.25-$.50 Blinds: No-Limit Cash Game.

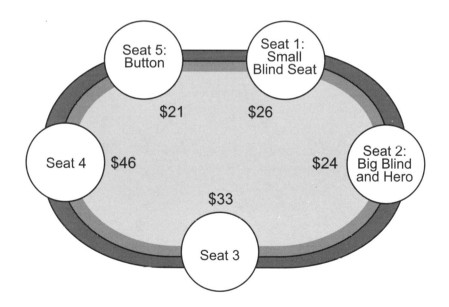

Seats 4 and 5 each limp into the pot. The small blind calls and you get to see a free flop from the big blind with 7♣ 6♥. The flop comes J♠ 8♦ 5♣. The small blind checks and you do the same. The cutoff bets $2, the button calls, and the small blind folds. There is $6 in the pot. What do you do?

Answer: You have an open-ended straight draw giving you 8 outs, which are about 5 to 1 against improving on the next card. You are only getting 3 to1 pot odds, but also have some considerable implied pot odds with two remaining opponents. The implied pot odds make this a reasonable call. Call.

In the actual hand the player called. Everyone checked when the 3♣ fell on the turn. The river was the 9♦. The big blind bet out $3 and got one caller who showed 5♥ 4♠.

Note that this player won $9 with his $2 call. His call resulted in 4.5 to 1 implied pot odds. Bases on the results of the hand, his effective implied pot odds were not justified given the 5 to 1 odds against improving. The effective implied pot odds are not always as high as they seem.

$0.5-$1 Blinds: No-Limit Cash Game.
You hold 7♥ 6♠ in the big blind with a stack of $90. The under-the-gun player limps, as does the cutoff. Three players see the flop of Q♠ T♠ 9♠. You check and the player in early position goes all-in for $55. The cutoff folds. There is $58.50 in the pot. What do you do?

Answer. This example demonstrates an important No-Limit concept - you should rarely draw to hands that do not have a high likelihood of winning if you hit. In this example, you have both a flush draw and a gut-shot straight draw but neither one gives you a very good hand. If you hit your flush, anyone with a spade higher than a 6 beats you. If you hit your straight, anyone with a J or flush beats you. Fold.

$.50-$1 Blinds: No-Limit Cash Game.

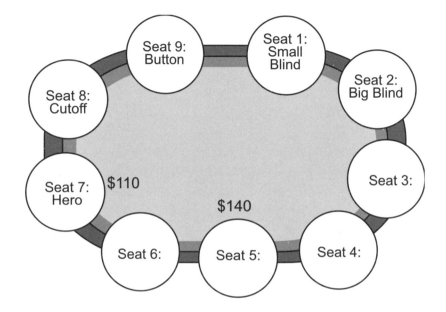

Seat 5 calls and you raise from Seat 7 to $4 with A♥ A♠. Everyone else folds and two players see the flop of 9♣ 8♦ 2♣. Seat 5 checks. There is $9.50 in the pot. How much do you bet?

Answer: Drawing hands that your opponent could be sitting on include a flush draw, a draw to trips or two pair, or a straight draw. There are a lot of scary cards that could come on the turn. I would make a decent size bet of about ¾ the size of the pot to give my opponent poor odds to call. Bet $7.

In the actual hand the player bet $5 and his opponent folded. I prefer to bet half the pot when the board is less scary. The scarier the board, the more I tend to bet to protect my hand. With a bet of $5, you are giving your opponent about 3 to 1 pot odds, which are decent pot odds if holding a flush or straight draw. A bet of $7 forces your opponent to pay a slightly higher price for his draw.

$0.5-$1 Blinds: No-Limit Cash Game.

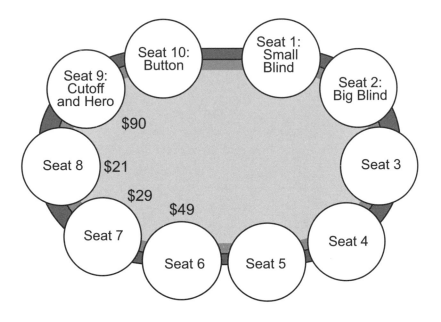

You are in the cutoff and are dealt A♠ Q♠. Seat 6 raises to $4. The next two players call and you decide to call. Four players see a flop of J♠ T♠ 6♥. The pre-flop raiser bets $5. Seat 7 raises all-in to $25. Seat 8 calls all-in for $17. There is $64.50 in the pot. What do you do?

Answer: This is a lot of heat for a No-Limit game. Flops that hold a couple of high cards like JT can often generate a lot of action. Your opponents could be holding a set, two pair, straight draws, flush draws, and big pairs. However, you hold the nut flush draw along with a nut gut-shot draw. Given all the action, I would not place too much value on the two over-cards. Therefore, you could possibly have 12 nut outs. However, there is a decent possibility that you are either against a set and/or another flush draw given all the action. If you are against a set, the 6♠ would not win the hand for you. If you are against another flush draw, you only have 7 flush outs instead of 9. If you discount down to 9 douts, you are 2 to 1 against improving. Faced with a $25 call you are getting 2.5 to 1 pot odds. With two opponents already all-in you are getting good pot odds to call.

The question now becomes how to play the hand against the pre-flop raiser. You can either call to encourage your opponent to stay in the hand or raise to try and drive him out of the pot. This is a large pot so you should determine whether raising would have any benefits. A raise might get an opponent to fold hands such as AK, AJ, or AT. You might even be able to get a hand like KK to fold with all of this action. You improve your chances of winning a large pot by driving out these hands. For example, if a Q comes, you could win the whole pot if you can get AK or KK to fold. Of course, there is no guarantee as you could still lose to one of the opponents who are all-in.

Alternatively, you might consider calling to encourage your opponent to stay in the pot. This improves the pot odds on your draw. It is a close decision but I would lean towards calling. It is unlikely that you would win anyhow with your overcards given that you are against two all-in opponents. The $45 in your opponent's stack is a significant amount of money to keep in the pot to improve your pot odds on your draw. If your opponent decides to raise you all-in, you are risking $45 to win $104.50, which is right at 2.3 to 1 pot odds. In either case playing your hand is profitable. Call.

In the actual hand, the player moved all-in and the pre-flop raiser folded. Two blanks hit the board and Seat 7 won the pot with top two pair.

$0.25-$.50 Blinds: No-Limit Cash Game.
A player from middle position with $110 in his stack raises to $2. You decide to only call from the cutoff with KK and $82 in your stack. The button calls and three players see the flop of Q♦ 4♥ 2♣. The middle

player checks, you bet $2, the button folds and the middle player raises to $6. You decide to slow-play and just call. The turn card is the 3♠. The middle player bets $6. There is $24.75 in the pot. What do you do?

Answer: You have a very strong hand. At this point your biggest worry is a hand like QQ, AA, or possibly a small set. Given the action so far, you must feel confident with your hand. There is a good chance that you are against a hand like AQ, KQ, or QJ. AQ is somewhat of a concern as your opponent now has nine outs, which are about 4 to 1 against improving. You should bet an amount that forces your opponent into making a mistake with insufficient pot odds to call. To calculate the break-even point we get:

$(\$24.75 + x)/x = 4.1$

$24.75 = 3.1x$

$x = \$8.98.$

By raising an additional $9, your opponent would be getting 33.75/9 or 3.8 to 1 pot odds. His hand is 4.1 to 1 against improving. Of course, your opponent is also getting implied pot odds since you will call some bets on the river. Therefore, you must raise more than this minimum amount to force your opponent into a mistake. I would raise to somewhere around $25, which would give your opponent about 2.6 to 1 pot odds. Raise to $25.

In the actual hand, the player only called and an ace came on the river. His opponent bet $6 and the player lost when his opponent showed AQ. It is critical to protect your hand and force your opponent into making mistakes when they have draws. Note that this player made mistakes on all three streets by not adequately protecting his KK. He gave his opponent decent effective implied pot odds on every street to make his draw.

$1-$2 Blinds: No-Limit Cash Game.

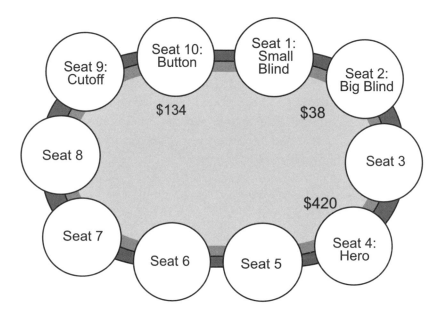

Seat 3 limps and you limp behind him with 8♠ 7♠. Three middle players call and the button raises to $8. The big blind calls and everyone else calls. Great game! Seven players see the flop of Q♠ 4♠ 4♣. The button bets $15 and the big blind check-raises all-in to $30. There is $102 in the pot. You and the button each have over $100 left in your stack. What do you do?

Answer: You are 4 to 1 against improving on the next card and are receiving about 3.3 to 1 pot odds. Your outs need to be discounted since there is a pair on the board giving your opponents full-house possibilities. You also are not drawing to the best flush draw. It is possible that you are drawing dead or close to it. You also face the possibility that the button will re-raise and put you all-in should you decide to call. This is an easy decision. Fold.

Continuing with the above hand. You call and the button calls. The turn is the A♦. You check and your opponent bets $25. There is now $172 in the pot. What do you do?

Answer: A $25 bet into a $147 pot is a rather weak bet. Your opponent either has a monster or is rather weak. If he does not hold AA or QQ, you have nine outs, which are about 4 to 1 against improving, and you are getting 6.9 to 1 pot odds. Remember though, there is a side pot that you might not win if the big blind has either a full-house or better flush draw. Still, with this large pot, I would be inclined to call now given the pot odds. Hold'em is a game of tough decisions and the weak call on the flop put you in a situation where you must make a difficult decision. Although a full-house or better flush draw is a possibility, you cannot always assume the worst. Call.

In the actual hand, the player called and missed his flush. The button showed A♠ Q♥ and the big blind K♣ T♣. Great game!

$.50-$1 Blinds: No-Limit Cash Game. You limp from early position with T♦ 8♦ and $51 sitting in front of you. The next early player has $44 in chips and raises to $3. You call and two players see the flop of J♦ 9♣ 3♦. You check and the early player bets $10. There is $17.50 in the pot. What do you do?

Answer: You have 15 outs to a flush and open-ended straight draw, which is better than even money to improve by the river. You are 2 to 1 against improving on the turn card. With this large draw, it is at least an easy call. But with big draws, you should always consider the option of raising. You are the favorite to win this hand. Therefore, even if you go all-in and are called, you are getting good pot odds on your money. In addition, there is a lot of money in the pot that you might win right away by moving all-in. Move all-in and force your opponent to either fold or put in his remaining $31. Go all-in.

In the actual hand, the player only raised to $20 and his opponent called.

Continuing with the above hand... You make the mistake of allowing your opponent to continue rather cheaply. The turn card is the 3♠. You check and your opponent moves all-in for $21. There is $68.50 in the pot. What do you do?

Answer: Your poor play has put you in a position where you will have to improve your hand in order to win the pot (versus giving yourself a chance to win the pot on the flop by moving all-in). First evaluate whether or not you can make this draw. The pot odds are 3.3 to 1. The odds against improving your hand are 2 to 1 (31 bad cards versus 15 good cards). This is an easy call.

Realize that if you were going to call an all-in bet on the turn, a much better play would have been to move all-in on the flop in order to give your opponent a chance to fold. With big draws such as this one, you should always look for a strategy that would give your opponent a chance to fold on either the flop or turn. Call.

Note that pushing a drawing hand versus a lone opponent should often be considered. In contrast, as we discussed previously, you should often consider building a side pot in multiway pots if the short stacks are already all-in. The exception to this is when driving out the remaining opponent can significantly improve your chances of winning a large pot.

In the actual hand, the player called and found himself against 88 giving him three more outs. The A♦ came on the river and he won a nice size pot. This time he was lucky but you must be aggressive to be successful in Hold'em.

$.05-$.10 Blinds: No-Limit Cash Game.
In a passive cash game you decide to limp first-in from middle position with 9♠ 7♠. You have $5 in your stack. The cutoff calls holding $15 in his stack. Three players see the flop of Q♠ 9♥ 3♠. You bet $.40 and the cutoff raises to $.80. You have noticed that the cutoff always moves all-in with a set or better. There is $1.55 in the pot. Assume that your opponent has at least a pair of queens or better. What do you do?

Answer: You are getting 3.9 to 1 pot odds. You have a flush draw and five outs to two pair or trips for a total of 14 outs. 14 outs are 2.4 to 1 against improving on the next card. You are getting good pot odds to at least call.

You should also consider raising given this strong draw. 14 outs is even money to improve by the river. Given this board and the play of your opponent, there is very little discount required on your outs. Therefore, even if you moved all-in and are called, you are getting decent pot odds given the money already in the pot. In addition, there is a chance that your opponent will fold and you will win the pot without a challenge. Be aggressive and move all-in. Go all-in.

In the actual hand, the player called and hit his flush on the turn. He moved all-in and his opponent called with A♠ Q♥. The flush stood up taking home a nice pot.

Tournament Hands

No-Limit Sit-n-Go. Level VII. $150-$300 Blinds.

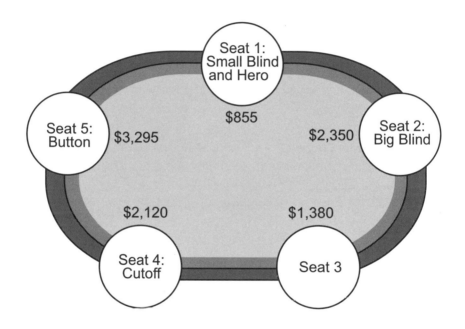

Seat 3 raises to $600. You are short-stacked in the small blind with J♦ 8♠. There is $1050 in the pot. What do you do?

Answer: Seat 3 has a low stack but is not yet desperate. With $1,380 in chips, this player will only have $930 in chips after paying the blinds. Advanced players understand that this is likely the last opportunity to win a pot uncontested and will raise with practically any hand. Most opponents, however, are more conservative and would wait for a decent hand before raising. Therefore, I would assume that your opponent has at least a respectable hand.

J♦ 8♠ is a slight favorite (51.5%) against a random hand. Assuming the raiser has better than a random hand, you are a likely underdog. Another risk in this hand is that the big blind has yet to act. You are most likely an underdog against the initial raiser and if the big blind jumps into the hand you will be a big underdog. The pot odds of moving all-in are 1.6 to 1, as you would be risking $705 to win $1155. Although you are short-stacked, you still have a few more hands to try and wait to find a more profitable opportunity. Also note that with $855, you still have some folding equity that might give you a chance to win a pot uncontested. Fold.

In the actual hand, the player folded. The big blind woke up with KK and the early player showed AQ.

$30 No-Limit Sit-n-Go. Level VI. $100-$200 Blinds.

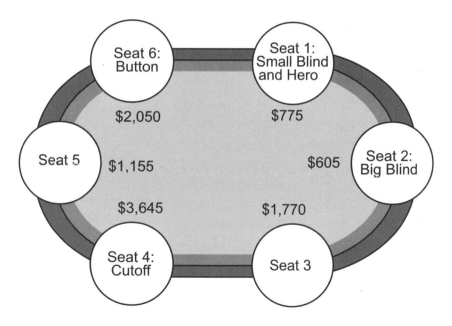

It is folded to you in the small blind and you look down at A♦ 3♥. You have $675 in chips left and the big blind has $405 remaining. There is $300 in the pot. What do you do?

Answer: The first thing to realize is that your opponent is practically pot-committed. By moving all-in, you would be giving your opponent 2 to 1 pot odds to call, as there would be $805 in the pot with your opponent facing a $405 call. Even a hand like 63 off-suit is getting 2 to 1 pot odds against a random hand (assuming the big blind thinks you would raise with any hand). A♦ 3♥ is a 56% favorite against a random hand. Given that you are a slight favorite and that there is already $300 of dead money in the pot, go all-in.

In the actual hand, the player simply limped in.

Continuing the above hand. The small blind limps and you look down at 8♥ 4♣. There is $400 in the pot. What do you do?

Answer: If there is a small chance that you could steal the pot then a raise could be a profitable play. 8♥ 4♣ will win 37% of the time against a random hand, so the probability that your opponent will fold does not need to be very high to try and steal this pot. However, you are very low in chips. Even by going all-in, your opponent is getting sufficient pot odds to call, as you would be offering him 2 to 1 pot odds. Only a weak opponent without a good understanding of probabilities and pot odds would fold in this situation. Given the small probability that you will get your opponent to fold, I would take the free flop and see how the hand develops. Check.

In the actual hand, the player raised and was called by the small blind.

No-Limit Sit-n-Go. Level V. $50-$100 Blinds.

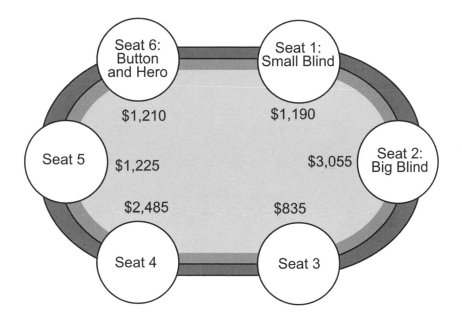

Seat 3 limps for $100. Seat 5, a loose player, raises to $700. You are on the button with J♣ J♦. There is $950 in the pot. What do you do?

Answer: Your opponent is a loose player so he could playing with a wide range of hands in this situation. His raise is quite large which gives the impression that he does not want to be called. This effectively lowers the probability that he is holding a premium hand. JJ is the 4th best Hold'em hand so you are most likely a good favorite against this opponent. One other consideration is that you have two opponents yet to act behind you; however, you have a premium hand and must act accordingly. Move all-in and hope for the best.

In the actual hand, the player moved all-in. His opponent showed AK and hit a pair on the flop. Loose players get good hands also but you were still a small favorite in this hand.

$30 No-Limit Sit-n-Go. Level VII. $150-$300 Blinds.

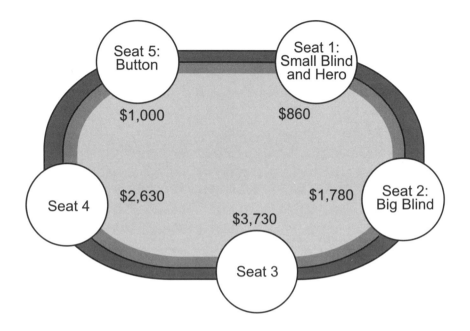

Seat 3 limps for $300. The button moves all-in for $1000. You are in the small blind and look down at TT with only $710 chips remaining. There is $1750 in the pot. What do you do?

Answer: You are getting 2.5 to 1 pot odds and hold a high middle pair. You must respect the raiser's hand somewhat as he is making a stand against a limper who is also the big stack. On the other hand, the raiser has a low stack and is in a situation where he must take some type of stand quite soon. Therefore, you can put him on a wide range of possible raising hands. You are the low stack and must make a move yourself before being blinded away. You probably will not find a better time than with TT so move all-in and hope for the best. Go all-in.

In the actual hand, the player called and his hand held up against A♣ 3♥.

No-Limit Tournament. Level V. $75-$150 Blinds.

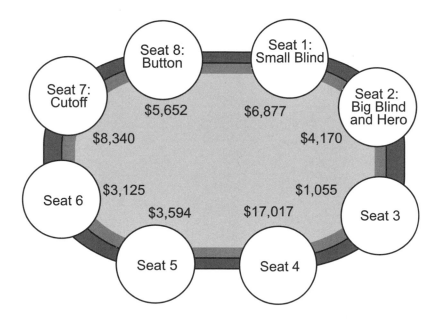

Seat 4, Seat 5, the button, and the small blind all call. You hold 4♦ 3♦ in the big blind and check. Five players see the flop of J♦ 5♠ 2♥. You check and the player in Seat 4 bets $300. Everyone folds to you. There is $1050 in the pot. What do you do?

Answer: You are getting 3.5 to 1 pot odds and are almost 5 to 1 against improving to the nut straight. The flop is a rainbow making this a very strong draw. A call is an easy decision given the implied pot odds. You are hoping for an ace in the hopes that your opponent is sitting on AJ. Of course, a 6 would not be too bad either. Call.

In the actual hand, the player called and both players checked the turn. The player hit the nut straight on the river and won a huge hand, as his opponent was slow-playing two pair.

$30 No-Limit Sit-n-Go. Level 1. Blinds are $10-$15.

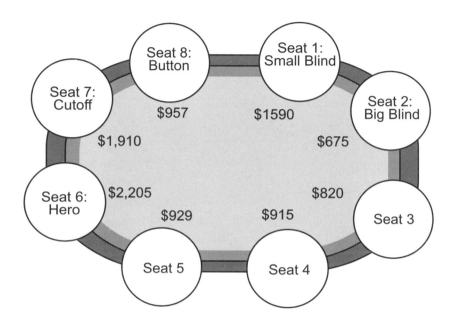

You are the chip leader in Seat 6. Seat 4 calls and you raise to $75 with A♣ Q♣. The cutoff, button, and the early limper all call. There is $325 in the pot and four players see the flop of J♦ T♣ 7♣. Seat 4 checks and you bet $160. Only the cutoff calls and the 9♦ falls on the turn. You bet $150 and the cutoff raises to $500. There is $1,295 in the pot. What do you do?

Answer: You are getting 3.7 to 1 pot odds ($1,295/$350). You have 12 strong outs to the nut flush and nut gut-shot draw. If you are against a set, you only have 10 outs since the J♣ and 9♣ are no good. 10 outs are 3.6 to 1 against improving. In either situation you are getting the correct pot odds to call and will still probably pick up some additional bets on the river if you hit your hand. Call.

In the actual hand the player called and the K♠ fell on the river. The player went all-in, was called, and won a huge pot. His opponent showed 8♣ 5♣.

Another perspective of the hand above.

Assume you are the player with the straight on the turn. How much would you need to raise to ensure that your opponent is not getting correct pot odds to call?

Answer: Your opponent has $1,820 in chips after his $150 bet on the turn. You have $1675 remaining in your stack. There is $795 in the pot. Given the board and the size of the pot, it will be difficult to get away from this hand on the river so you stand to lose your entire stack should your opponent hit a big hand.

If your opponent holds JJ, he has 10 outs to a full-house. If he has A♣ K♣ or A♣ Q♣, he has 10 outs to a higher flush or straight. 10 outs are 3.7 to 1 against improving. Using simple algebra you can determine the correct amount to raise.

$$X = (795 + 1675)/3.7 = \$667$$

Therefore, you need to raise $667 to $817 for your opponent to call with break-even odds. In this case, your opponent would have to call $617 for the chance to win $2,470 ($795 + $617 + $1,058 which is the amount remaining in your stack). By raising to at least $817, you ensure that your opponent is not making a profitable call. Raise to at least $817.

Realize that I am not advocating that you have to fully protect your hand every time. In the above scenario we are assuming the worst case. There are many hands that your opponent might be holding that you would still welcome a call. The probability that he holds the best draw is actually quite low given all of the possible hands with which he might still call.

There are situations where you take calculated risks in Hold'em to try and win bigger pots. For example, by raising to $500, you are hoping that your opponent calls with many weak hands where he is not getting correct pot odds to call. Of course by doing this, you assume the risk of giving your opponent correct odds should he have a big draw. If the likelihood of a big draw is high, you should be more concerned with protecting against it.

$30 No-Limit Sit-n-Go. $100-$200 blinds.
Seven players remain. A short-stacked player moves all-in for $735 under-the-gun. Everyone folds to you in the big blind. You are also short-stacked with $455 after posting the big blind. There is $1035 in the pot and you look down at A♠ T♣. What do you do?

Answer: You are getting over 2 to 1 pot odds in this situation. A♠ T♣ is about 2.5 to 1 to win even against big pocket pairs such as KK or QQ. Your opponent is short-stacked so he could be on a wide range of hands. Your hand could be the favorite and, if not, you are getting decent pot odds to improve to the best hand. Call.

In the actual hand the player called and hit a straight.

No-Limit Tournament. $1500-$3000 Blinds with $150 ante.

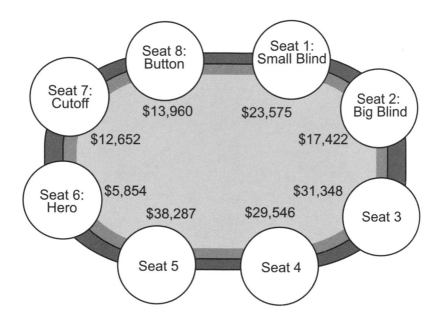

Seat 3 limps for $3000 and it is folded to you in Seat 6 with Q♥ J♥. What do you do?

Answer: You only have four more hands until you must pay the big blind. By then you will be pot-committed to play any hand. It is always best to try and get your money into the pot before another opponent but Q♥ J♥ is a pretty good hand. You also do not have enough folding equity to steal the blinds so you are going to be forced into a showdown no matter what over the next few hands. With another caller already in the hand, this could be a good opportunity to try and double or triple up. Raise all-in. In the actual hand the player moved all-in. The button moved all-in for $13,810 and everyone else folded. The button had TT and won with a straight.

$30 No-Limit Sit-n-Go. Blinds $30-$60.

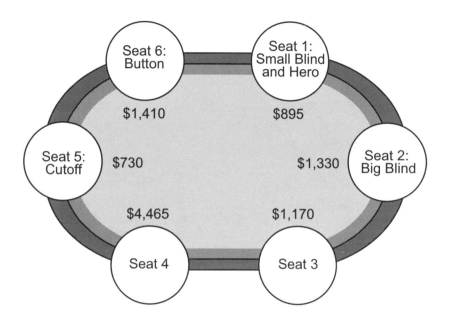

The big blind appears to be a rather standard, unimaginative player. He has not been involved in any pot of significance up to this point. You are dealt Q♠ 8♠ in the small blind. Seat 4 limps in. You limp and 3 players see the flop of 5♠ 4♣ 2♠. All three players check. The turn is the 6♥. You bet $120 and the big blind raises to $240. The middle player folds. There is $540 in the pot. What do you do?

Answer: This raise looks like your opponent is begging for a call. It appears that your opponent has a straight so trying a semi-bluff re-raise is unlikely to work. However, given that the raise is so small you should consider whether or not drawing to the flush is profitable. You have nine outs, which are about 4 to 1 against improving. You are getting 4.5 to 1 pot odds making this an easy call, especially when considering the extra bets you would win if you hit your hand. Call.

In the actual hand the player called and completed a flush when the 3♠ fell on the river. The player bet out $210 and was called taking home a pot of $1080. The big blind showed J♥ 3♦. Although the player won this hand with his draw, he probably could have earned more chips. It is hard for an opponent to fold with a straight on the board even though a flush is a possibility. It takes a very strong player to make those kinds of lay-downs. Most players at this limit would call an all-in bet.

$30 No-Limit Sit-n-Go. $50-$100 Blinds.

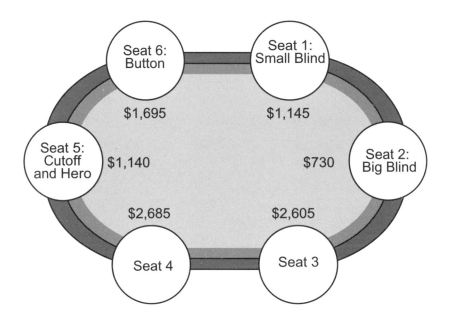

Seat 4 raises to $200. You make a questionable call with TT (moving all-in is a strong consideration in this situation). The small blind moves all-in. It is folded to you. There is $1645 in the pot. What do you do?

Answer: First determine the probability that your opponent holds a pocket pair greater than TT's, the probability that he has a pair less than TT's, and the probability that he has over-cards. According to our chart on page 182, *Probability of a Raiser Holding a Pocket Pair Given a Range of Hands*, there is a 47% chance your opponent has a pocket pair 88 or higher if we assume he would raise with 88 or higher or AK-AJ or higher. This is probably a decent assumption given this particular scenario. The probability is actually a little less since we know that you have TT in your hand. For simplicity's sake, assume that 45% of the time he has a pocket pair and 55% of the time he has two over-cards. Breaking down the 45%

of the time when he holds a pocket pair, 30% of the time he will hold AA-JJ and 15% of the time 99 or 88 (these percentages are not exact but I have thrown out TT as a possibility since you would just split the pot).

The probability that you will win is calculated as follows:
.55 (.53) + .30 (.20) + .15 (.80) = 0.47 or 47%.

You face a $940 bet to win $1645 making this an easy call. In coin flip situations you are often correct to call given the amount of money already in the pot. Call.

In the actual hand, the player called and won against 66. It looks like your opponent was even more aggressive with pairs then we estimated which increased your probability of winning this hand even more.

In reality it is difficult to put an opponent on an exact range of hands. You can never be certain so you should estimate this in your calculations. For example, in this hand, you might give small pairs a small probability given your impression of your opponent. The calculations can get quite complicated so we make our best estimates. In my "answer" to this problem, the important thing is to understand the process one goes through in determining the probability that your hand will win rather than worrying about whether or not you agree with the range of hands I chose for the opponent.

An estimate range of 45-55% of winning this hand seems pretty reasonable and is close enough to give us the information we need to make a good decision.

As a final comment, calling pre-flop with TT put this player in a difficult situation. We would rather not have to battle two over-cards. Moving all-in in this type of situation puts pressure on your opponents to make a tough decision and gives you the chance of picking up the pot without a fight. Of course it worked out nicely in this spot to be against an all-in player holding 66.

$30 No-Limit Sit-n-Go. Blinds $100-$200.

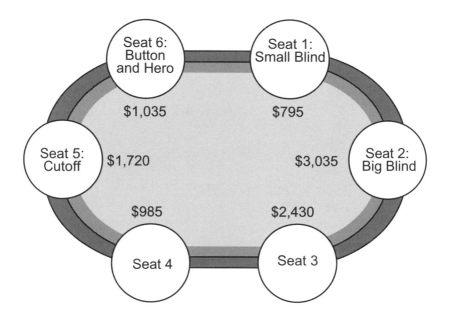

Seat 5 raises to $400. You are on the button with 8♣ 8♥. There is $700 in the pot. What do you do?

Answer: With only $1,035 in chips, you are pretty much pot-committed if you decide to play your hand. Therefore, the only options are whether or not you should move all-in or fold. By moving all-in, it is unlikely you will get your opponent to fold since he will be getting pot odds to call with just about any hand. You also have to worry about two more opponents left to act, one of whom could have a premium hand.

If we look at the chart on page 180, *Probability of a Raiser Holding a Pocket Pair from Each Position*, we see there is a 22% chance of your opponent holding a pocket pair from late position. Your opponent's small raise seems to indicate that he does not want to risk too much with his hand so there is a decent possibility it is not too strong unless he is slow-playing a premium pair. A 20% probability of your opponent holding a pocket pair greater than 88 is reasonable (most opponents would raise a little more with pairs lower than 88 to try and get their opponents to fold so we disregard this possibility for this analysis).

Therefore, .2(.20) + .8 (.53) = 0.46. By moving all-in you will have about a 46% chance of winning this pot against the cutoff. What are the pot odds? You are risking $1,035 to win $1,335 so the pot odds are 1.3 to 1 and the chance that you will win is 1.2 to 1 against. The pot odds are slightly in your favor so going all-in has a positive expectation against the cutoff.

However, there is also a chance that the small blind or big blind will jump into the pot with a premium hand. In this case, the probability that they have a pocket pair is much higher since they would be playing against a raiser and a re-raiser. This would lower your overall expectation. This is probably a break-even decision or slightly less. The main problem is that you do not have enough chips to get the cutoff to fold; otherwise, moving all-in would probably have a good positive expectation.

Since this is about a borderline decision in terms of odds, the decision should now focus on tournament strategy. The blinds are $100-$200 so it costs $300 just to pay the blinds every six hands. This does not give you much time to wait for a premium hand. You also get rewarded for tournaments by finishing in the top spots. Getting blinded away reduces the chance that you can get your chip stack into a good position to challenge the leaders. Overall this looks like a pretty good opportunity to double-up and make a move in this tournament so I would move all-in. Go all-in.

Continuing the Hand Above from a different player's perspective.
The button moves all-in and you now assume the role of the big blind who holds A♦ 3♦. You sense weakness in the cutoff and are pretty sure you can get him to fold his hand by moving all-in. The button has played solid

poker, although a little on the loose side, so you believe he might move all-in with hands like KQ, KJ, Ax, and possibly QJ. You draw the line on any hand worse than KJ or QJ. There is $1,735 in the pot and it will cost you $1,035 to call. What do you do?

Answer: You are getting 1.7 to 1 pot odds. Let us estimate a 25% chance of your opponent holding a pocket pair, 25% of Kx or worse, and 50% chance of Ax (these are approximate based on the possible combinations).

Our expectation is therefore:
.25 (.35) + .25 (.60) + .50 (.33) = 0.40 or 40%.

You are about 1.5 to 1 against winning and are getting 1.7 to 1 pot odds. Although this looks like a decent opportunity, you cannot be sure that the cutoff will fold. Although you might sense weakness, you cannot be sure. If the cutoff is sitting on a big hand, you will be a big underdog. This is not a situation to risk your chip position to double up an opponent when you are against both a pre-flop raiser and a player who has moved all-in. Look for a better opportunity rather than calling with a relatively weak hand. Fold.

In the actual hand, the big blind called and knocked out his opponent on the button.

No-Limit Tournament. $100-$200 Blinds.
The cutoff raises to $600 and has a stack of $4,130. You call in the big blind with A♦ 2♦ and a stack of $3910. The flop comes 9♦ 9♥ 6♦. You check and your opponent bets $600. There is $1900 in the pot. What do you do?

Answer: You are getting 3.2 to 1 pot odds. Your flush draw is about 4 to 1 against improving on the turn. If your ace is good, you have 12 outs, which are 3 to 1 against improving. You could even hit your 2, which might be the best hand. The flush is a big draw so you are getting pretty good implied pot odds. If you call, your opponent might be afraid that you are sitting on trips and could check the turn giving you a free card. You have been presented with a good situation that warrants at least a call.

Check-raising your opponent is also a good option. By check-raising you give yourself a chance to win the pot immediately. The downside to check-raising is that you are pretty much committing yourself to the pot given your stack size. However, it is likely that you have at least 12 outs and possibly even more. Even with only 12 outs, you are close to even money on winning the hand with two cards to come and your pot odds are good given the money already in the pot. Against a solid opponent, I like check-raising to put the pressure on my opponent. Against a weaker opponent, I might take a more conservative approach by just calling hoping to improve my hand without risking a lot of chips. Call or raise.

In the actual hand, the player called. Both players checked the turn and the player made an additional $200 on the river when she hit her flush.

No-Limit Tournament. Level III. $25-$50 Blinds.

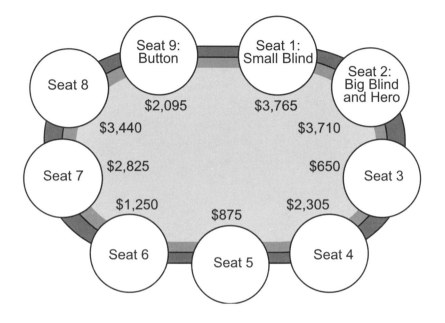

Seat 4, 5, and 8 all call. You hold T♣ 9♦ in the big blind and check. Four players see the flop of Q♣ J♦ 4♣. You check. Seat 4 bets $100 and the other two opponents call. There is $525 in the pot. What do you do?

Answer: You are getting 5.25 to 1 pot odds. You have an open-ended straight draw giving you 8 outs. However, there are two clubs on the board making two of your outs quite weak. Given that this is No-Limit, you have enough ammunition to protect your hand on the turn should you hit your draw. There is also the risk that you could hit your straight with a K only to lose to AT. Given the flush possibilities, higher straight possibilities, and redraws, I would discount my outs down to five douts. Five douts is 8 to 1 and you have 5 to 1 pot odds. The question is now how much do you think you can win if you hit your hand? Since there are several opponents in the hand you have good implied pot odds to call.

Once you decide that you are going to at least call, the next decision is whether or not to raise. One problem with raising in this situation is that you would be giving your opponent a chance to re-raise and knock you out of this strong draw. Calling ensures that you will be given the possibility of hitting a big hand. Call.

In the actual hand, the player called and hit the nut straight on the turn.

Continuing with the hand above.
You call and the 8♦ comes on the turn. You must act first and decide to bet out. What amount will ensure that each opponent is not getting correct odds to call?

Answer: There is $625 in the pot. If an opponent has a flush draw, he has eight outs given that you already have one of the flush cards in your hand. If your opponent has a set, he has 10 outs. With 10 outs out of 46 cards, your opponent is 3.6 to 1 against improving (36 blanks divided by 10 outs). To calculate the break-even bet amount for the worst case you get:
$$(\$625 + x)/x = 3.6$$
$$625 = 2.6x$$
$$x = \$240.$$

You need to bet more than $240 to ensure that each opponent is not getting correct pot odds to call. Realize however that you are against several opponents so collectively they could be holding a club flush draw, a diamond flush draw, and a full-house draw. In this case, the cumulative outs of your opponents are very dangerous. Each additional caller will also give the following opponent better pot odds. Another problem is that you will be acting first on the river, which could put you into a tough predicament given so many possible scare cards. I would bet an amount somewhere close to the amount in the pot to put pressure on your opponents and charge them a hefty price for continuing with the hand. $240 is the answer but bet the pot.

In the actual hand, the player bet $250 and everyone called. The 6♥ came on the river. The player bet $225 and was raised all-in by Seat 5 who held 44. Going back to the flop call of $100, the player ended up winning the $525 in the pot on the flop, an additional $750 on the turn, and $475 more on the river. The implied pot odds turned out to be pretty good.

No-Limit $30 Sit-n-Go. Level VI. $100-$200 Blinds.

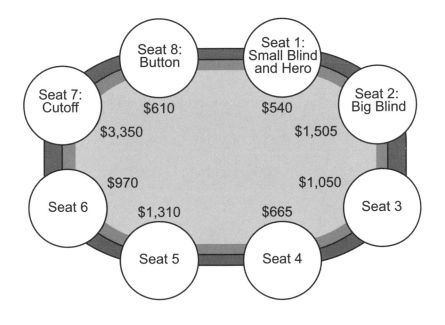

Seat 3 moves all-in for $1050. It is folded to you in the small blind with Q♣ J♣. You only have $440 in chips remaining. You have the possibility of winning $840 of what is in the $1350 pot. What do you do?

Answer: You must risk $440 to win $840 giving you 1.9 to 1 pot odds. Seat 3 is not in a must-raise situation (for the typical player) so you should respect the raise and assume you are most likely an underdog; however, it is difficult to fold a decent hand when you are getting almost 2 to 1 pot odds. Another consideration is that you still have the big blind lurking behind you.

Although the pot odds are decent, the next question to ask is whether or not this is the best time to make a move. One should try to be the raiser rather than the caller whenever possible. However, with only $440 in chips, you do not have enough folding equity to steal the blinds so you are destined to end up in a showdown. Another factor to consider is that there is still a chance you will get a premium hand dealt to you before the blinds come around again. Of course, if you get dealt a premium hand later it would be nice to have some chips to play it with. It is a close decision but I would gamble and go all-in. Go all-in.

In the actual hand, the player called and beat 88 when a Q fell on the flop.

No-Limit $30 Sit-n-Go. Level VI. $100-$200 Blinds.

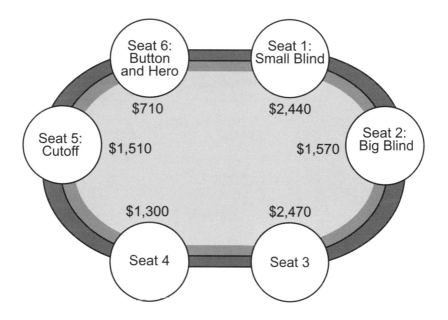

Seat 4 raises to $650. You are on the button with Q♥ J♥. There is $950 in the pot. What do you do?

Answer: The middle player has indicated strength by raising so you are most likely the underdog. There are also two opponents acting behind you who might wake up with a big hand. Calling is a weak play when you are most likely the underdog. Although Q♥ J♥ looks pretty, you still have a few more hands to try and find a situation where you would be the favorite. You also have enough chips on the next couple of hands to get everyone to fold should you raise first-in.

This hand is similar to the previous hand example but there are enough subtle differences to make this hand a fold. Fold.

In the actual hand, the player moved all-in and doubled up when he hit a straight on the turn.

Charts and Stats

This section of the book should serve as an excellent resource to help you learn some key stats and probabilities that will help you make better decisions at the poker table. For example, it is important to know in a tournament how often your hand would win against a random hand. You can also learn generalizations such as how often two over-cards will beat two under-cards. How often does an under-pair beat an over-pair? If you are holding an ace, what are the odds that you will win if your opponent holds a pocket pair? The charts will also show you the likelihood of your opponent holding a pocket pair when he has raised. These extensive charts are intended to be a reference guide for you for the years to come.

For each chart, we will look at how some of the stats were calculated. The actual calculations are not necessarily important, but they are given as a reference nevertheless. I have tried to be comprehensive in the stats and probabilities that are presented but if you need to calculate something on your own you ought to be able to do so by learning from the example calculations. Note that the stats give the probability of a win or tie.

Numbers, stats, and probabilities are pointless unless they are helpful in making better decisions. Following each chart is a section on how the particular stat can be applied to certain situations you might face at the table.

Starting Hands

Probability of Being Dealt a Specific Starting Hand

	Probability	Odds[23]
AA	.0045	220 to 1
KK	.0045	220 to 1
Etc.	.0045	220 to 1
AKs	.003	331 to 1
AK off-suit	.009	110 to 1
Any AK	.012	82 to 1
Any 32	.012	82 to 1
Any Pocket Pair	.059	16 to 1
Suited Cards	.235	3.3 to 1
Others (Off-suit)	.706	.4 to 1
Connectors	.157	5.4 to 1
Suited Connectors	.039	25 to 1

Overview

This chart looks at the probability of being dealt specific starting hands. In total, there are 1326 different starting hands…52×51/2×1. In reality there are only 169 unique starting hands when it comes to strategy. In other words, J♣ J♦ is the same as J♠ J♥, so there are many duplicates within the 1326 various starting hands that can be dealt. This chart looks at what is important - how often will you receive AA rather than how often you receive A♣ A♦.

---

[23] The odds given in these charts are calculated using the rounded probability number. This could result in small discrepancies between what is shown and the actual odds, although the difference is irrevalent in terms of strategy.

The Calculations

Calculating the probability of receiving a specific hand such as AA is rather straightforward. There are four aces in the deck giving you a 4/52 chance of receiving an ace for your first card and a 3/51 chance at an ace on your second card. The chance that both of these occur is 4/52 × 3/51 which is .0045 of the time or 220 to 1 against occurring. AKs is even rarer since on the second card you have to match the exact suit of the first card. This calculation is 8/52 × 1/51, which equals .003% of the time or 331 to 1 against occurring.

When calculating the probability of being dealt a pocket pair, the first card is given. Matching this card is a 3/51 chance, which equals .059 or 16 to 1. Suited cards are similar in that the first card is given and then you have a 12/51 chance of matching your suit, which equals .235 or 3.3 to 1. Calculating the probability of being dealt an off-suit hand that is not a pair is just a process of elimination: 1.0 - .059 - .235, which equals 0.706.

For connectors, once you are dealt the first card, there are four cards above and four cards below that connect[24]. Therefore, 8/51 gives you 0.157. For suited connectors, there is only one card above and one card below that connect and match the suit. This gives us 2/51 or 0.039.

Application

This chart does not necessarily help us with strategy, but the numbers help us with the mental approach to this game. The numbers clearly show that we do not see premium hands very often. When you only receive AA on average once every 221 hands, you can see why you have to be quite patient in this game. Even if you are playing on the Internet where the action is much faster, you will still only see AA about once every three hours in a full ring game. You can only expect to see AA, KK, or QQ about once an hour on the Internet. When you are playing in a live game, these time periods can be doubled since the action is so much slower. By knowing how rare it is to actually receive various hands, hopefully you will be able to stay patient during your dry runs rather than starting to go on tilt.

---

[24] This is true even for an ace, which can have a K below or a 2 above.

Probability of Being Dealt a Quality Starting Hand

	Probability	Odds
Two Cards K or Higher	.021	47 to 1
Two Cards Q or Higher	.05	19 to 1
Two Cards J or Higher	.091	10 to 1
Two Cards T or Higher	.143	6 to 1
Pairs 22 to 99	.036	27 to 1
Raise First-in from Early[25]	.041	23 to 1
Limp First-in from Early	.032	30 to 1
Total First-in from Early	.073	13 to 1
Raise First-in from Middle	.071	13 to 1
Limp First-in from Middle	.029	33 to 1
Total First-in from Middle	.10	9 to 1
Raise First-in from Late	.162	5 to 1
Limp First-in from Late	0	N/A
Total First-in from Late	.162	5 to 1

Overview

This chart gives an idea on how often we receive quality starting hands to play. How we define "quality" is relative to each player, the type of game we are in, and what position we are in. The first stats indicate how often we receive high cards and pairs. The purpose of these stats is not to argue whether or not QT off-suit is a quality hand but rather to give you an indication to how often you will receive high cards.

---

[25] These probabilities are based on the starting hand guidelines from my first book, *Internet Texas Hold'em*. These guidelines are provided in the Appendix.

From a strategic perspective, one can argue that from early position in an un-raised pot you could always play any two cards Q or higher, with possibly the exception of KQ off-suit in some games. From middle position in an un-raised pot, two cards J or higher are usually playable. From late position, you could play any two cards T or higher in an un-raised pot. If you added pairs 22 through 99, you can add 3.6% to each position to come up with a total percentage.

The next set of stats is more specific for each position in terms of actual strategy during a Hold'em game. These stats follow the starting hand guidelines provided in my book *Internet Texas Hold'em*[26]. These stats tell you how often you would be able to enter the pot first-in when following the guidelines in my book. For those who track their stats online, you should be able to compare the percentages that you actually play to those that I recommend when first-in.

The Calculations
The probability of being dealt two cards J or higher is calculated as follows: There are 16 cards J or higher of the 52 cards in the deck. This gives us a 16/52 chance of receiving one of those cards with the first card. After being dealt one of those cards, you then have a 15/51 chance of being dealt another one. Multiplying these together we get $16/52 \times 15/51$ = 0.091 or 9.1%.

For the calculations such as *Raise First-in from Early*, I used the charts in *Internet Texas Hold'em*. I first determined the probability of receiving a specific pair, two suited cards, and two off-suit cards. Then going to the charts, I determined how many hands met the conditions for raising first-in. For each pair I added .0045, for each suited hand .003, and for each off-suit hand .009. Once all the hands are added together you get the probability for each position.

---

[26] Note that the starting hand guidelines in the book were intended for beginning to intermediate players. Advanced players can and often will play a few more hands than the guidelines I provide and would raise in more situations. Also, the starting hand guidelines are intended for limit games.

Application

These stats show just how rare it is to receive a quality starting hand. In practice, you should only be playing about 15% to 25% of your starting hands in a full limit Hold'em ring game depending on the type of game you are in and what type of player you are. Advanced players in very loose games might play slightly more than that but generally playing more that 25% of your hands indicates a leak in your game.

When you are in a game where 4 to 5 opponents are seeing every flop you are in a great game! What hands could these players be playing? The key is to remain patient. Also note how often you should be raising first-in from each position. This percentage goes up dramatically the closer you are to the button.

Here is an interesting exercise to try at home that will show you just how weak your opponents' starting hands generally are. Deal ten hands face up and then start playing each hand as you would pre-flop. If you follow tight starting hand guidelines, you will see that it is rather common for everyone to fold to a raiser. You will rarely see flops with more than two players. In fact, seeing a flop with four players is very rare! Yet, this is what we now typically see in most games.

Now try playing hands a little more "loosely" than you would normally play. For example, many weak opponents like Ax and one-gapped suited connectors. You will still have a hard time dealing hands with 5 players seeing the flop on a consistent basis. Once you realize just how weak your opponents' hands typically are, you will realize how much of an advantage you have over your opponents by keeping a tight pre-flop hand selection.

Probability of a Raiser Holding A Pocket Pair from Each Position

Raisers	Probability	Odds
Early	.333	2 to 1
Middle	.319	2.1 to 1
Late	.222	3.5 to 1
Small Blind	.360	1.8 to 1
Big Blind	.428	1.3 to 1

Re-raisers	Probability	Odds
Early	.529	.9 to 1
Middle	.529	.9 to 1
Late	.456	1.2 to 1
Small Blind	.529	.9 to 1
Big Blind	.529	.9 to 1

Overview

This chart gives you the probabilities that a raiser is holding a pocket pair in his hand. This was calculated by looking at all of the combinations of possible raising hands according to the Starting Hand guidelines in *Internet Texas Hold'em*[27]. Once all combinations were determined, I then calculated what percentage represented pocket pairs compared to other raising hands such as AK. The assumption is that the player is either first-in or facing a lone limper.

The Calculations

A pair has six different possible combinations. For example, A♦ A♥, A♦ A♣, A♦ A♠, A♥ A♣, A♥ A♠, A♣ A♠. Non-pair hands such as AK, suited or off-suit, have 16 different combinations. A hand such as AKs only

---

[27] Note again that the guidelines in *Internet Texas Hold'em* were intended for limit games.

has 4 different combinations. For each position, I determined the total number of pair combinations listed as raising hands. For example, in early position, my charts indicate that you ought to raise with AA, KK, or QQ, which results in 18 different pair combinations. This compares to 36 combinations for AKs, AK, AQs, AQ, and AJs listed as raising hands from early position. 18/54 gives us .33 or 33% of the time someone is holding a pocket pair while raising from early position.

Application
When a player raises indicating strength we are always in a predicament of trying to determine whether or not our opponent has a large pocket pair or just AK. When we hit a pair on the flop we have to try and determine our best strategy against the raiser. These stats show that it is actually more likely that our opponent is holding two high cards rather than a pocket pair.

You can see that re-raisers have about a 50% chance of holding a big pocket pair compared to two big cards such as AK or AQ.

Realize that these guidelines follow my starting hand charts. All players certainly do not play the same way and many players do not follow my starting hand guidelines. You will need to adjust accordingly. Is the player likely to raise with pairs lower than what is indicated in the Starting Hand charts? What about non-pair hands that are ranked lower than what I recommend? If the player is likely to raise more hands in general, I suspect the percentage of pairs will still remain close to those indicated in this chart.

Probability of a Raiser Holding A Pocket Pair Given A Range of Hands

Range	Probability	Odds
AA, KK, AK	.429	1.3 to 1
AA-QQ, AK-AQ	.360	1.8 to 1
AA-JJ, AK-AJ	.333	2 to 1
AA-TT, AK-AQ	.484	1.1 to 1
AA-TT, AK-AJ	.385	1.6 to 1
AA-88, AK-AJ	.467	1.1 to 1
Any pair, AK-AT, KQ	.494	Even
Any pair, Ax, KQ-KT, QJ	.234	3.3 to 1

Overview

This chart looks at the probability of your opponent holding a pocket pair given a range of hands that you feel your opponent may have. You can see that based on the ranges provided that it is rare to find a situation where there is more than a 50% probability that your opponent is holding a pocket pair. In the situation where you put your opponent on a wide range of hands like Ax and QJ, there is only a 23% chance that your opponent holds a pocket pair. When you put a player on AA, KK, or AK, the probability is still only .429 that he holds a pocket pair.

The Calculations

First look at the easiest scenario and then just build from there for the other calculations. There are 16 combinations of AK, six combinations of AA and six combinations of KK for a total of 28 combinations. 12 of these are pairs so there is a 43% chance of your opponent holding a pocket pair.

Application

These charts can give you a good indication of whether or not you are against an over-pair when holding a small pocket pair. Playing hands like TT-88 are quite difficult when the pot is raised as you are unsure where you stand. Using these charts we can make some estimations on how our hand might stack up.

For example, assume you hold 66 and your opponent puts you all-in at a critical stage in the tournament. It is crunch time and you need to decide whether or not to gamble. You can quickly determine the probability of a win using these charts. Let us look at AA-TT, AK-AJ. There is a 38% chance your opponent holds a pocket pair. Therefore, there is a 62% chance he does not. We can make some generalizations that an under-pair is a 4 to 1 underdog against an over-pair and has roughly even odds against two over-cards. Therefore, the probability your hand will win is computed as follows:

.38 (.20) + .62 (.50) = 0.39.

You have a 39% chance of winning the hand, which is 1.6 to 1. Now all you have to do is compare this to the pot odds to determine whether a call is profitable or not.

An interesting hand came up in the 2004 Borgata Open between Josh Arieh and Phil Ivey. The blinds were $12K-$24K with $3K antes. A player in middle position raised to $80,000. Josh called with 33 and Phil Ivey moved all-in with $403K. The middle player folded and it was up to Josh. There was $581K in the pot. What would you do?

This is an excellent example to show how to use probabilities to determine whether a call is profitable or not. When watching the broadcast, my initial reaction was that Josh should fold. He was either in a coin flip situation against two over-cards or a big underdog against a big pocket pair. But Josh also had pot odds on his side. The question is whether or not they were enough.

Josh is faced with a $323K call to win $581K, giving him 1.8 to 1 pot odds. What are the various hands Phil Ivey could be holding? I have never played Phil Ivey, so I only have information about his style that I have gathered from watching him on TV. The player who initially raised had enough chips remaining that Phil probably thought he could get him to fold to an all-in reraise unless his opponent was sitting on a premium hand. Given that Josh called, Phil was probably thinking that Josh was weak and would fold his hand. Therefore, Phil's main concern was the original raiser.

Phil had a below average stack and needed to make a move so this offered a good spot. However, I believe he also respected the original raiser so he would not make this play without a quality hand. The range of hands that I suspect Phil might move in here include AK, AQ, and all pairs TT or higher. Our chart shows that there is a 48% chance of him holding a pocket pair given this range of hands (30 pairs divided by 62 total combinations).

For simplicity, let us assume 50% of the time Phil holds an over-pair in this situation and 50% of the time two over-cards. A pair of 3's will win about 18.5% of the time against an over-pair and about 53% of the time against two over-cards. We can now calculate the expectation of this bet.

Against an over-pair: $.185(581) - .815(323) = -156$
Against two over-cards: $.53(581) - .47(323) = 156$

Given that we estimated an even chance of holding an over-pair or two over-cards, it turns out that calling is a break-even proposition. Now we know what Mike Sexton meant during his broadcast when he said that Josh was faced with a tough decision! Since we have a break-even play right here, the question now becomes, do you risk doubling up Phil Ivey, one of the best poker players in the world, or should you try and knock him out now? Phil was acting right behind Josh and I'm sure Josh would try anything to get Phil out to improve his chances on later hands. Josh decided to call and Phil was knocked out of the tournament.

Note that if we felt Phil might raise with a few more pairs than we would have a negative expectation on this call. If we felt he might raise with hands like AJ or KQ then the expectation would be slightly positive. In either case, the decision was quite close to a break-even proposition.

The Flop

Probability of Hitting Certain Hands on the Flop

	Probability	Odds
Two suited cards hitting a flush	.008	124 to 1
Two suited cards hitting a flush draw	.11	8 to 1
Two cards such as AK flopping trips	.014	70 to 1
Two cards such as AK hitting two pair	.021	47 to 1
Two cards such as AK hitting at least one A or K	.324	2.1 to 1
Any pocket pair hitting at least a set	.118	7.5 to 1

Overview

This chart shows how infrequently we will hit some of our starting hands on the flop. Even AK is a 2 to 1 underdog on hitting a pair. This is obviously the same for any two cards hitting a pair on the flop where one of the flop cards matches your pocket cards.

The Calculations

Consider just a few of these calculations and you ought to get the idea on how to calculate the others. What are the odds of hitting a flush on the flop when holding two cards of the same suit? There are 50 unknown cards and each card on the flop must match our suit. There are 11 suited cards left in the deck. Therefore, we have an 11/50 chance that the first card matches our suit, a 10/49 chance on the 2nd card, and a 9/48 chance on the 3rd. Multiplying these together we get:

$11/50 \times 10/49 \times 9/48 = 0.008$ or close to 1%.

What about hitting a flush draw? The odds the first card matches our suit remains 11/50 and the 2nd 10/49. However, now the 3rd card must be a different suit or 39/48. Multiplying these together gives us the probability of two suited cards flopping when the 3rd card is a blank, which is 0.0365. There are two other scenarios to consider however. The blank could come on the 1st card in addition to it coming on the second. The three scenarios are (where B is a blank): XXB, XBX, and BXX. Therefore, 3(.0365) = 0.1095 or close to 11%.

To calculate the probability of hitting trips we have three scenarios:
A or K, complete trips, blank (do not hit full-house or quads)
A or K, blank, complete trips
Blank, A or K, complete trips

$6/50 \times 2/49 \times 44/48 = 0.0045$
$6/50 \times 45/49 \times 2/48 = 0.0046$
$46/50 \times 6/49 \times 2/48 = 0.0047$

Total = 0.014 or a little more than 1%

Similar for trips, the calculation for two pair is:
$6/50 \times 3/49 \times 44/48 = 0.0067$
$6/50 \times 45/49 \times 3/48 = 0.0069$
$46/50 \times 6/49 \times 3/48 = 0.0070$

Total = 0.02 or 2%

The following calculation looks at a very common scenario: the odds of a pocket pair hitting at least a set[28]. An easy way to look at this is to calculate the probability of not hitting a card matching our pair. For example, if we hold AA, there is a 48/50 chance of not hitting an ace on the first card. There is a 47/49 on the second and a 46/48 for the third. $48/50 \times 47/49 \times 46/48 = 0.8824$. Since there is a .8824 probability of not hitting an ace, we can conclude that there is a .1176 chance that we do hit an ace, which is 7.5 to 1.

---

[28] A full-house where the flop is three-of-a-kind is not included in this calculation.

Application

The main point that you should get from this chart is that Hold'em is a game of patience. You can see why suited cards are not so valuable unless your hand has other merit such as having high cards or straight possibilities. You will rarely flop a flush and you are 8 to 1 against even flopping a draw. On those rare cases where you flop a draw, you still have your work cut out for you, as you are about 2 to 1 against hitting your flush by the river. Stay patient with your starting hand selection.

Also realize that a good starting hand is only good until you see the flop. Many times you will start out very strong and the flop will offer no improvement. AK can be a very disappointing hand when it only offers you improvement about once every three flops. Instead of thinking of AK as a premium hand, think of it as a drawing hand to ensure you do not push it too aggressively at the wrong times.

Probability of Flopping a Straight

Flopping a Straight	Probability	Odds
AK, AQ, AJ, AT, K9, Q8, J7, T6, 95... 84, 73, 62, A5, A4, A3, and A2	.003	332 to 1
KQ, KJ, KT, Q9, J8, T7, 96, 85, 74, 63... 52, 42, 32	.007	142 to 1
QJ, QT, J9, T8, 97, 86, 64, 53, or 43	.010	99 to 1
JT, T9, 98, 87, 76, 65, or 54	.013	76 to 1

Overview

This chart looks at the probability of flopping a straight for connectors, 1-gapped, 2-gapped, 3-gapped, and hands which do not *stretch* like AQ and A3[29]. You can see that flopping a straight is a rare occurrence. Hands that include an ace do not have as many straight possibilities since they can only go in one direction. These are basically the same as any 3-gapped starting hand.

The Calculations

The following looks at the probability of completing a 3-gapped straight

- ♣ If you hold AT, you need to hit KQJ in some combination to complete your straight.
- ♠ There are 50 remaining cards in the deck. The probability that you get a K, Q, or J on the first card is 12/50.
- ♦ The probability that you get one of the remaining cards next is 8/49.
- ♥ Finally, you have a 4/48 chance of completing the straight.
- ♣ $12/50 \times 8/49 \times 4/48 = 0.003$ or 332 to 1.

---

[29] Note that we have assumed your starting hand is off-suit so straight flushes are not included as a possibility. If your hand is suited, this chart shows how many straights and straight flushes you would hit.

A 2-gapped hand has one additional straight opportunity so it can complete 2 different straights. Therefore, 2 (12/50 × 8/49 × 4/48) = 0.006 or 142 to 1.

A 1-gapped hand can make three different straights. Therefore, 3 (12/50 × 8/49 × 4/48) = 0.0098 or 99 to 1.

Finally, a hand like JT, which can make the maximum number of four straights is calculated as 4 (12/50 × 8/49 × 4/48) = 0.013 or 76 to 1.

Application
It is apparent from these charts that flopping straights is quite rare. The strength in connectors comes from the probability of flopping draws. Note how gaps impact the odds of hitting a straight. A hand like JT or 76 has four different possible straights it could hit. For example, JT will hit a straight with AKQ, KQ9, Q98, and 987. Compare this to a 3-gapped hand such as K9, which can only hit a straight with QJT. These stats show why connectors are so much more valuable than gapped starting hands.

Probability of Flopping an 8-Out Straight Draw

Flopping an 8-Out Straight Draw	Probability	Odds
KQ, KJ, KT, Q9, J8, T7, 96, 85, 74, 63... 52, 42, or 32 (no double belly-busters)	.031	31 to 1
QJ, QT, J9, T8, 97, 86, 75, 64, 53, or 43 (includes one double belly-buster)	.065	14 to 1
JT, T9, 98, 87, 76, 65, or 54 (includes two double belly-busters)	.10	9 to 1

Overview
This chart looks at the probability of flopping an 8-out straight draw for connectors, 1-gapped, 2-gapped, and hands which do not stretch like AK. The stats assume that you do not hit a straight on the flop. An 8-out straight draw includes both open-ended straight draws and *double belly-buster* draws.

Calculation
Straight draws become a little more complicated because we need to be sure not to double count any of the combinations. In this example, we will look at JT and all of its combinations.

First, calculate the probability of flopping an open-ended draw with a flop of KQx or QKx when you hold JT. For now, assume that x does not complete a straight and that the board is not paired.
- ♠ The probability that a K or Q falls on the first card is 8/50.
- ♦ The probability is then 4/49 that we complete the draw on the next card.
- ♥ We then have a 34/48 chance of hitting a blank (missing the straight and not pairing the board).

♣ In the above bullet, 34 is the number of cards we are counting as blanks so we are excluding 3 kings, 3 queens, 4 aces, and 4 nines (48-14 = 34).

♦ We will count combinations where the board is paired later.

♦ Therefore, the probability of hitting KQx or QKx = $8/50 \times 4/49 \times 34/48 = 0.01$.

The KQ combination can come in different order on the flop: KQx, KxQ, QKx, QxK, xKQ, and xQK. The calculation for the other combinations is as follows:

♥ We could hit a K or Q on the first card, hit a blank on the 2nd, and then get our draw on the last card.

♣ This calculation is $8/50 \times 35/49 \times 4/48 = 0.01$.

♠ Finally we could hit a blank first, hit a K or Q and then complete the draw, which is $36/50 \times 8/49 \times 4/48 = 0.01$.

So far we have not included any combinations when the board is paired.

♣ We can also get our open-ended draw when the board is as follows: KKQ, KQK, KQQ, QQK, QKQ, and QKK.

♠ The calculation for each is $(4 \times 4 \times 3)/(50 \times 49 \times 48) = 0.0004$.

♦ There are six different combinations so the calculation is $6 (4\times4\times3)/(50\times49\times48)) = 0.002$.

Summarizing the above we get:

K or Q, complete the draw, and a blank $8/50 \times 4/49 \times 34/48 = 0.01$
K or Q, a blank, and complete the draw $8/50 \times 35/49 \times 4/48 = 0.01$
A blank, K or Q, and complete the draw $36/50 \times 8/49 \times 4/48 = 0.01$
Pairing such as KKQ (six possibilities) $6 (4\times4\times3)/(50\times49\times48) = 0.002$

Total = 0.031

Now that we have the probability for a specific draw we can simply multiply this by the number of possible draw combinations for each hand:

♦ The 2-gapped straight draws like T7 or a hand like KQ have only one possible combination so the probability is .031.

♠ A 1-gapped draw or a hand like QJ has two possible combinations. For example, with QJ, we could hit with KT or T9. Therefore, 2 × .031 = 0.06.

♣ Finally, a no gapped draw with maximum straights like JT or 65 is 3 × .031 = 0.09.

We should also add the possibility of double belly-buster draws since from a strategic perspective it is the same as an open-ended straight draw. For example, with JT, if you flop K97 or AQ8 you have the equivalent of an open-ended draw. The probability of flopping K97 is 12/50 × 8/49 × 4/48 = 0.0033. For hands that have one double belly-buster draw, add 0.0033 + 0.062 for a total of 0.065. For hands like JT with two double belly-buster draws, add 2(.0033) + 0.093 for a total of 0.10.

Application

These odds show how connectors start to add some value to your hand. Realize however that you have a 9 to 1 chance of hitting a strong draw, which is still 2 to 1 against completing by the river. Connectors by themselves are of little value. However, once you consider the straight, pair, two-pair, and trip possibilities you have a reasonable starting hand in the right conditions. Note that you can also flop gut-shot draws that sometimes add additional value to your hand.

Probability of Flopping a Straight or 8-Out Straight Draw

Flopping a Straight or Straight Draw	Probability	Odds
AK, AQ, AJ, A4, A3, A2	.003	332 to 1
3-Gapped hands: AT, K9, Q8, J7, T6, 95... 84, 73, 62, A5	.006	166 to 1
KQ, KJ, KT, Q9, J8, T7, 96, 85, 74, 63... 52, 42,or 32	.038	25 to 1
QJ, QT, J9, T8, 97, 86, 64, 53, or 43	.075	12 to 1
JT, T9, 98, 87, 76, 65, or 54	.113	8 to 1

Overview

This chart looks at the probability of flopping a straight, open-ended straight draw, or a double belly-buster draw. The chart looks at connectors, 1-gapped, 2-gapped, and hands which do not stretch like AK.

Calculations

The two previous charts looked at straights and 8-out straight draws. Each of these is independent of the other, so we can simply add the probabilities together to find the total probability of hitting a straight or strong straight draw.

Application

This chart clearly shows the value of connected hands over gapped hands. A hand like KQ or J8 does not have very many possibilities for hitting a straight. A connected hand like JT will hit either a straight or strong draw about 11% of the time. Once you add in the possibilities of hitting trips, two pair, or one pair, you start to realize the value of your hand. If your hand is suited, you now have even more value.

Realize, however, that these are still speculative hands. Hitting a draw on the flop is one thing, but the odds are still against you for completing your draw. You generally need a lot of callers in the hand with a low risk of a raise in order to play off-suit connectors in Limit Hold'em. The higher connectors like AK and KQ are worth a lot more than the lower connectors even though they have fewer straight opportunities since most of the value in these hands comes from hitting a high pair.

One of the reason pros like the middle connectors in No-Limit so much is that their hand is relatively disguised. These hands have the potential of hitting big hands to double-up. Also, since they are medium cards, you rarely lose big pots since you will not tend to get married to your hand as much as you would with a hand like AK.

Probability of Flopping at least one Over-card to a Pocket Pair
(and you do not hit a set)

	Probability	Odds
KK	.21	3.8 to 1
QQ	.38	1.6 to 1
JJ	.52	.9 to 1
TT	.63	.6 to 1
99	.72	.4 to 1
88	.78	.3 to 1
77	.82	.2 to 1
66	.85	.17 to 1
55	.87	.15 to 1
44	.88	.13 to 1
33	.88	.13 to 1
22	.88	.13 to 1

Overview

This chart looks at the probability of flopping at least one over-card to your pocket pair. Since we are trying to assess the probability of an unfavorable flop, we do not include those flops where we hit a set and an over-card falls, as this is an ideal situation. You can see that the probability is so low to get all under-cards with a hand like 44 that the probability is basically the probability against hitting a set.

Calculations

We will look at one example, JJ, as they are all pretty similar. The combinations are given below:

♥ An over-card, any card other than a J, any card other than a J
♣ No over-card or J, an over-card, any card other than a J
♦ No over-card or J, no over-card or J, an over-card

The calculation is as follows:
$12/50 * 47/49 * 46/48 = 0.22$
$36/50 * 12/49 * 46/48 = 0.17$
$36/50 * 35/49 * 12/48 = 0.13$

Total = 0.52 or 52%

Application

This chart shows how vulnerable a pocket pair is to having an over-card come on the flop. Even a hand like QQ runs a 38% risk of an unfavorable flop. An over-card does not always indicate that your hand will lose but it is definitely not a situation where we feel comfortable. These stats should emphasize the importance of raising our premium pocket pairs. It is a shame to let a hand like AT see a flop cheaply when we are holding a strong hand like QQ. Make your opponents pay a price for chasing weak hands.

These stats also show how the medium pockets pairs are generally not worth much unless you hit a set. Even a pair like TT has a 63% chance of seeing an over-card on the flop. If you are playing a loose limit Hold'em game and it is difficult to isolate, you generally should try to keep as many opponents in the hand as possible in hopes of hitting a set. The more opponents there are, the better your implied pot odds become. Also realize that even when you do manage to have a favorable flop, those medium pairs are still vulnerable on the turn and river to over-cards.

River

Probability of Hitting Certain Hands in a Showdown

	Probability	Odds
Two suited cards hitting a flush with exactly 3 cards matching your suit on the board	.06	16 to 1
Any pair hitting at least a set	.19	4 to 1
Two cards such as AK hitting at least one A or K	.51	Even
Two cards such as AK hitting trips[30]	.03	32 to 1
Two cards such as AK hitting two pair[31]	.056	17 to 1

Overview
This is a general chart looking at the probability of hitting certain hands in a showdown.

Calculations
To calculate the probability of a pocket pair hitting at least a set, we can calculate the probability of not matching our pocket pair and then subtract from 1. The calculation becomes:
$$1 - (48/50 \times 47/49 \times 46/48 \times 45/47 \times 44/46) = 0.19$$

Calculating the probability of AK hitting at least one A or K is similar to calculating a pocket pair hitting a set. Calculate the probability of not hitting an ace or king and then subtract from 1. The calculation becomes:
$$1 - (44/50 \times 43/49 \times 42/48 \times 41/47 \times 40/46) = 0.51$$

---

[30] This scenario looks at hitting at least AA or KK without hitting a full-house or four-of-a-kind. Straights and flushes with the three blank cards are included.

[31] This calculation looks at hitting two pair by matching both of your dealt cards. Aces and kings are used in this example. A board such as A5532 is not included. If you hold 65, a board such as 65KKT is included.

There are 10 combinations of AK within the five board cards. The calculation of hitting two pairs is as follows:

$10 \times (6 \times 3 \times 44 \times 43 \times 42)/(50 \times 49 \times 48 \times 47 \times 46) = 0.056$

To interpret the above calculation, you have three aces or three kings which could be dealt on the first card for a total of six cards. Once you hit an ace or king, there are three cards left to complete your two pair. Once you have hit two pair, the next card cannot complete a full-house, so there are 44 blanks left within the remaining 48 cards. There are then 43 blanks of the 47 remaining cards and 42 blanks out of the 46 on the river. This calculation looks at receiving AK on the first two board cards. However, these can be arranged in 10 different combinations with five cards so we multiply by 10.

Application
Realize that sometimes you will be folding on the flop or turn so you will not hit these hands as often as these probabilities might indicate.

The odds of hitting a flush are an interested statistic. Another way to look at this is that you will hit a very strong hand about 6 times out of 100 versus just an off-suit hand. These additional pots often make the difference between folding and calling. Realize also that the pots you win with flushes are usually large pots.

These stats show why playing trash hands is a risky proposition. The odds of hitting a good hand like two pair or trips are just too great to justify investing additional money with hands like 73 and 92. This point is especially noteworthy when you consider that you often have to play to the turn or river in order to hit two pair or trips.

AK is a valuable starting hand because you are going to hit a strong hand at least 50% of the time and sometimes you will win unimproved, as your opponent must have at least a pair to beat you.

Showdown Charts in Heads-up Situations

Overview

The following charts show how various hands match up against specific hands or against random hands when played to a showdown. They are organized as follows:

- ♥ Pairs in various scenarios
- ♦ High cards in various scenarios
- ♣ Miscellaneous hands in various scenarios
- ♠ All 169 starting hands versus a random hand

One of the main applications of these stats is to help make all-in decisions before the flop when either you or your opponent is short-stacked.

Calculation

All of these calculations can be replicated using the Poker Odds calculator found on my website at www.InternetTexasHoldem.com. The calculator is able to:

1. Compare any hand versus any other hand
2. Compare a hand versus a random hand
3. Compare a hand versus any range of hands

Application

Although quite difficult to memorize all of the stats in these charts, you can start to make some generalizations about how certain hands match-up. I suggest learning some of the more common scenarios that you will find yourself in[32]:

- ♣ Over-pairs win about 80% of the time against an under-pair. An under-pair wins about 20% of the time.

---

[32] The numbers given in these bullets are generalizations based on the overall range of hands given in the scenario. The actual number will depend on the exact hands in the scenario. Some of the factors that impact the numbers include whether or not you and your opponent share cards of the same suit and the number of straight possibilities a specific hand can hit.

- ♠ A pair is generally a small favorite versus two over-cards, although this depends on the exact cards. The odds are so close that these types of situations are generally considered to be coin-flip situations.
- ♠ A pair versus two under-cards is between a 4-to-7 to 1 favorite. Suited middle connectors are close to the 4 to 1 stat while off-suit cards with few straight possibilities are close to 7 o 1.
- ♥ Pairs versus an over-card and under-card are about a 2 to 1 favorite.
- ♦ Two over-cards versus two under-cards are between a 1.5-to-2 to 1 favorite.
- ♣ Two cards versus an over-card and an under-card, for example T8 versus K5, is about a 1.5 to 1 underdog. This can range from 2 to1 to practically a break-even situation depending on the exact cards.
- ♠ You need at least 98s, T8o, T7s, J7, J5s, Q5, Q2s, or any A, K, or pair to have a positive expectation against a random hand.

Each time you find yourself in an all-in situation before the flop, reference these charts afterwards to determine whether or not you made the correct decision from a probability perspective. Eventually you will start to get a better feel for when a call is justified or not.

Pairs: Heads-up to a Showdown

Summary

Pair vs.[33]	AA	KK	QQ	JJ	TT	99	88	77	66	55	44	33	22
An over-pair	NA	.18	.18	.18	.19	.19	.19	.19	.19	.19	.19	.19	.18
An under-pair	.81	.81	.81	.81	.81	.81	.81	.81	.81	.82	.81	.80	NA
Two suited over-cards	NA	NA	.54	.54	.54	.52	.52	.52	.51	.51	.50	.50	.49
Two off-suit over-cards	NA	NA	.57	.57	.57	.55	.55	.54	.54	.54	.53	.52	.52
A2 off-suit	.93	.71	.71	.71	.71	.70	.70	.70	.70	.70	.70	.69	.66
A2 suited	.88	.68	.68	.68	.68	.67	.67	.67	.67	.67	.66	.65	.62
Random Hand	.85	.82	.80	.77	.75	.72	.69	.66	.63	.60	.57	.54	.50

---

[33] All of these probabilities are averages. The exact hands will cause some small differences from these averages.

General Conclusions[34]

Pair vs.	Probability of Win	Approximate Odds
An over-pair	.18 to .20	4.3 to 1 underdog
An under-pair	.80 to .82	4.3 to 1 favorite
Two suited over-cards	.46 to .54	Even
Two off-suit over-cards	.48 to .57	1.1 to 1 favorite
Ace, under-card, suited	.65 to .68	2 to 1 favorite
Ace, under-card, off-suit	.68 to .72	2.3 to 1 favorite
Card matching your pair and an over-card	.59 to .70	2 to 1 favorite
Card matching your pair and an under-card	.78 to .93[35]	5.5 to 1 favorite
Suited connectors below pair	.77 to .82	4 to 1 favorite
Connectors below pair	.80 to .86	5 to 1 favorite

---

[34] The ranges presented in this chart may be slightly different than the averages indicated in the summary chart. This is due to exact hands being taken into account rather than averages.

[35] A♥ A♣ vs. A♦ 6♥ is .93, 5♥ 5♣ vs. 5♣ 4♣ is .78

AA vs.	Probability of Win	Odds
AKs	.88	7 to 1 favorite...
AK off-suit	.93	13 to 1
ATs	.87	7 to 1
Ax off-suit	.93	13 to 1
Ax suited	.88	7 to 1
KK	.82	4.6 to 1
TT	.81	4.3 to 1
KQs	.83	5 to 1
KQ off-suit	.87	7 to 1
65s	.78	3.5 to 1
72 off-suit	.88	7 to 1
32 off-suit	.87	7 to 1
Any pocket pair	.81	4.3 to 1
Suited connectors below AA	.79	4 to 1
Connectors below AA	.83	5 to 1
A Random hand	.85	6 to 1

KK vs.	Probability of Win	Odds
AA	.18	4.6 to 1 underdog
An under-pair	.81	4.3 to 1 favorite…
AKs	.66	1.9 to 1
AK	.70	2.3 to 1
AQs	.68	2.1 to 1
ATs	.67	2.1 to 1
Ax off-suit	.71	2.4 to 1
Axs suited	.68	2.1 to 1
TT	.81	4.3 to 1
QJs	.82	4.6 to 1
QJ off-suit	.86	6 to 1
65s	.78	3.5 to 1
72 off-suit	.88	7 to 1
32 off-suit	.86	6 to 1
Suited connectors below KK	.79	4 to 1
Connectors below KK	.83	5 to 1
A Random Hand	.82	4.6 to 1

QQ vs.	Probability of Win	Odds
An over-pair	.18	4.6 to 1 underdog
An under-pair	.81	4.3 to 1 favorite...
AKs	.54	1.2 to 1
AK off-suit	.57	1.3 to 1
AQs	.66	1.9 to 1
ATs	.68	2.1 to 1
Ax off-suit, except AK and AQ	.71	2.4 to 1
Ax suited, except AK and AQ	.68	2.1 to 1
TT	.82	4.6 to 1
QJs	.84	5 to 1
QJ off-suit	.89	8 to 1
65s	.78	3.5 to 1
72 off-suit	.88	7 to 1
32 off-suit	.86	6 to 1
Suited connectors below QQ	.79	4 to 1
Connectors below QQ	.83	5 to 1
A Random Hand	.80	4 to 1

JJ vs.	Probability of Win	Odds
An over-pair	.18	4.6 to 1 underdog
An under-pair	.81	4.3 to 1 favorite...
Two suited over-cards	.54	1.2 to 1
Two over-cards	.57	1.3 to 1
AJs	.65	1.9 to 1
AJ off-suit	.69	2.2 to 1
AT-2 off-suit	.71	2.4 to 1
AT-2 suited	.68	2.1 to 1
JTs	.82	4.6 to 1
JT off-suit	.87	7 to 1
65c	.78	3.5 to 1
72 off-suit	.88	7 to 1
32 off-suit	.86	6 to 1
Suited connectors below JJ	.79	4 to 1
Connectors below JJ	.83	5 to 1
A Random Hand	.77	3.3 to 1

TT vs.	Probability of Win	Odds
An over-pair	.19	4.3 to 1 favorite
An under-pair	.81	4.3 to 1 underdog
Two suited over-cards	.54	1.2 to 1
Two over-cards	.57	1.3 to 1
ATs	.65	1.9 to 1
AT off-suit	.69	2.2 to 1
A9-2 off-suit	.71	2.4 to 1
A9-2 suited	.68	2.1 to 1
T9s	.82	4.6 to 1
T9 off-suit	.87	7 to 1
65s	.78	3.5 to 1
72 off-suit	.88	7 to 1
32 off-suit	.86	6 to 1
Suited connectors below TT	.80	4 to 1
Connectors below TT	.84	5 to 1
A Random Hand	.75	3 to 1

99 vs.	Probability of Win	Odds
An over-pair	.19	4.3 to 1 underdog
An under-pair	.81	4.3 to 1 favorite
Two suited over-cards	.52	1.1 to 1
Two over-cards	.55	1.2 to 1
A9s	.66	1.9 to 1
A9 off-suit	.70	2.3 to 1
A8-2 off-suit	.70	2.3 to 1
A8-2 suited	.67	2 to 1
98s	.82	4.6 to 1
98 off-suit	.87	7 to 1
65s	.79	4 to 1
72 off-suit	.89	8 to 1
32 off-suit	.86	6 to 1
Suited connectors below 99	.80	4 to 1
Connectors below 99	.84	5 to 1
A Random Hand	.72	2.6 to 1

88 vs.	Probability of Win	Odds
An over-pair	.19	4.3 to 1 underdog
An under-pair	.81	4.3 to 1 favorite…
Two suited over-cards	.52	1.1 to 1
Two over-cards	.55	1.2 to 1
A8s	.66	1.9 to 1
A8 off-suit	.70	2.3 to 1
A7-2 off-suit	.70	2.3 to 1
A7-2 suited	.67	2 to 1
87s	.82	4.6 to 1
87 off-suit	.87	7 to 1
65s	.80	4 to 1
72 off-suit	.89	8 to 1
32 off-suit	.86	6 to 1
Suited connectors below 88	.80	4 to 1
Connectors below 88	.84	5 to 1
A Random Hand	.69	2.2 to 1

77 vs.	Probability of Win	Odds
An over-pair	.19	4.3 to 1 underdog
An under-pair	.81	4.3 to 1 favorite
Two suited over-cards	.52	1.1 to 1
Two over-cards	.54	1.2 to 1
A7s	.66	1.9 to 1
A7 off-suit	.70	2.3 to 1
A6-2 off-suit	.70	2.3 to 1
A6-2 suited	.66	1.9 to 1
76s	.82	4.6 to 1
76 off-suit	.87	7 to 1
62 off-suit	.87	7 to 1
32 off-suit	.86	6 to 1
Suited connectors below 77	.81	4.3 to 1
Connectors below 77	.85	6 to 1
A Random Hand	.66	1.9 to 1

66 vs.	Probability of Win	Odds
An over-pair	.19	4.3 to 1 underdog
An under-pair	.81	4.3 to 1 favorite…
Two suited over-cards	.51	Even
Two over-cards	.54	1.2 to 1
A6s	.65	1.9 to 1
A6 off-suit	.70	2.3 to 1
A5-2 off-suit	.69	2.2 to 1
A5-2 suited	.66	1.9 to 1
65s	.81	4.3 to 1
65 off-suit	.86	6 to 1
32 off-suit	.87	7 to 1
Suited connectors below 66	.82	4.6 to 1
Connectors below 66	.86	6 to 1
A Random Hand	.63	1.7 to 1

55 vs.	Probability of Win	Odds
An over-pair	.19	4.3 to 1 underdog
An under-pair	.82	4.6 to 1 favorite…
Two suited over-cards	.51	Even
Two over-cards	.54	1.2 to 1
A5s	.64	1.8 to 1
A5 off-suit	.67	2 to 1
A4-2 off-suit	.70	2.3 to 1
A4-2 suited	.66	1.9 to 1
54s	.81	4.3 to 1
54 off-suit	.86	6 to 1
32 off-suit	.88	7 to 1
Suited connectors below 55	.83	5 to 1
Connectors below 55	.88	7 to 1
A Random Hand	.60	1.5 to 1

44 vs.	Probability of Win	Odds
An over-pair	.19	4.3 to 1 underdog
33 and 22	.81	4.3 to 1 favorite…
Two suited over-cards	.50	Even
Two over-cards	.53	1.1 to 1
A4s	.63	1.7 to 1
A4 off-suit	.67	2 to 1
A3, A2 off-suit	.69	2.2 to 1
A3, A2 suited	.66	1.9 to 1
43s	.83	5 to 1
43 off-suit	.88	7 to 1
A Random Hand	.57	1.3 to 1

33 vs.	Probability of Win	Odds
An over-pair	.19	4.3 to 1 underdog
22	.80	4 to 1 favorite...
Two suited over-cards	.50	Even
Two over-cards	.52	1.1 to 1
A3s	.63	1.7 to 1
A3 off-suit	.66	1.9 to 1
A2 off-suit	.69	2.2 to 1
A2 suited	.65	1.9 to 1
32s	.84	5 to 1
32 off-suit	.89	8 to 1
A Random Hand	.54	1.2 to 1

22 vs.	Probability of Win	Odds
An over-pair	.18	4.3 to 1 underdog
Two suited over-cards	.49	Even
Two over-cards	.52	1.1 to 1 favorite...
A2 off-suit	.66	1.9 to 1
A2 suited	.62	1.6 to 1
A Random Hand	.50	Even

High Cards: Heads-up to a Showdown

AK suited vs.	Probability of Win	Odds
AA	.12	7 to 1 underdog…
KK	.34	1.9 to 1
Any pocket pair below AK	.48	1.1 to 1
AQ-2 suited	.71	2.4 to 1 favorite…
AQ-2 off-suit	.75	3 to 1
KQ-2 suited	.72	2.6 to 1
KQ-2 off-suit	.77	3.3 to 1
Any two under-cards (not paired or connected)	.67	2 to 1
Suited connectors below AK, which does not match AK suit	.62	1.6 to 1
Off-suit connectors below AK	.65	1.9 to 1
A Random Hand	.67	2 to 1

AK off-suit vs.	Probability of Win	Odds
AA	.07	13 to 1 underdog...
KK	.30	2.3 to 1
Any pocket pair below AK	.45	1.2 to 1
AQ-2 suited	.70	2.3 to 1 favorite...
AQ-2 off-suit	.74	3 to 1
KQ-2 suited	.71	2.4 to 1
KQ-2 off-suit	.76	3 to 1
Any two under-cards (not paired or connected)	.65	1.9 to 1
Suited connectors below AK	.60	1.5 to 1
Off-suit connectors below AK	.63	1.7 to 1
A Random Hand	.65	1.9 to 1

AQ suited vs.	Probability of Win	Odds
AA	.13	7 to 1 underdog…
KK	.32	2.1 to 1
QQ	.34	1.9 to 1
Any pocket pair below AQ	.48	1.1 to 1
AK suited	.29	2.4 to 1
AK off-suit	.30	2.3 to 1
KJ-2 suited	.63	1.7 to 1 favorite…
KJ-2 off-suit	.66	1.9 to 1
AJ-2 suited	.70	2.3 to 1
AJ-2 off-suit	.74	3 to 1
QJ-2 suited	.72	2.6 to 1
QJ-2 off-suit	.76	3 to 1
Any two under-cards (not paired or connected)	.67	2 to 1
Suited connectors below AQ, which does not match AQ suit	.61	1.6 to 1
Off-suit connectors below AQ	.65	1.9 to 1
A Random Hand	.66	1.9 to 1

AQ off-suit vs.	Probability of Win	Odds
AA	.07	13 to 1 underdog…
KK	.28	2.6 to 1
QQ	.30	2.3 to 1
Any pocket pair below AQ	.45	1.2 to 1
AK suited	.25	3 to 1
AK off-suit	.26	2.8 to 1
KJ-2 suited	.60	1.5 to 1 favorite…
KJ-2 off-suit	.64	1.8 to 1
AJ-2 suited	.69	2.2 to 1
AJ-2 off-suit	.73	2.7 to 1
QJ-2 suited	.71	2.4 to 1
QJ-2 off-suit	.75	3 to 1
Any two under-cards (not paired or connected)	.65	1.9 to 1
Suited connectors below AQ	.60	1.5 to 1
Off-suit connectors below AQ	.63	1.7 to 1
A Random Hand	.64	1.8 to 1

KQ suited vs.	Probability of Win	Odds
AA	.17	5 to 1 underdog…
KK	.14	6.1 to 1
QQ	.35	1.9 to 1
Any pocket pair below KQ	.49	Even
AK suited	.29	2.4 to 1
AK off-suit	.30	2.3 to 1
AJ-2 suited	.42	1.4 to 1
AJ-2 off-suit	.45	1.2 to 1
KJ-2 suited	.71	2.4 to 1 favorite…
KJ-2 off-suit	.75	3 to 1
QJ-2 suited	.72	2.6 to 1
QJ-2 off-suit	.76	3 to 1
Any two under-cards (not paired or connected)	.68	2.1 to 1
Suited connectors below KQ, which does not match KQ suit	.62	1.6 to 1
Off-suit connectors below KQ	.66	1.9 to 1
A Random Hand	.63	1.7 to 1

KQ off-suit vs.	Probability of Win	Odds
AA	.13	7 to 1 underdog...
KK	.09	11 to 1
QQ	.31	2.2 to 1
Any pocket pair below KQ	.46	1.2 to 1
AK suited	.24	3 to 1
AK off-suit	.25	3 to 1
AJ-2 suited	.40	1.5 to 1
AJ-2 off-suit	.42	1.4 to 1
KJ-2 suited	.70	2.3 to 1 favorite...
KJ-2 off-suit	.74	3 to 1
QJ-2 suited	.71	2.4 to 1
QJ-2 off-suit	.75	3 to 1
Any two under-cards (not paired or connected)	.66	1.9 to 1
Suited connectors below KQ	.60	1.5 to 1
Off-suit connectors below KQ	.64	1.8 to 1
A Random Hand	.61	1.6 to 1

Miscellaneous Hands: Heads-up to a Showdown

QJ suited vs.	Probability of Win	Odds
AA or KK	.18	4.6 to 1 underdog...
QQ	.16	5.3 to 1
JJ	.37	1.7 to 1
Any pocket pair below QJ	.50	Even
AK suited	.36	1.8 to 1
AK off-suit	.39	1.6 to 1
AQ or KQ	.30	2.3 to 1
AJ or KJ	.30	2.3 to 1
QT-2 suited	.70	2.3 to 1 favorite...
QT-2 off-suit	.74	3 to 1
JT-2 suited	.72	2.6 to 1
JT-2 off-suit	.76	3 to 1
Any two under-cards (not paired or connected)	.68	2.1 to 1
Suited connectors below QJ, which does not match QJ suit	.63	1.7 to 1
Off-suit connectors below QJ	.66	1.9 to 1
A Random Hand	.60	1.5 to 1

JT suited vs.	Probability of Win	Odds
AA, KK, or QQ	.20	4 to 1 underdog…
JJ	.18	5 to 1
TT	.39	1.6 to 1
Any pocket pair below JT	.52	1.1 to 1 favorite
Suited over-cards	.37	1.7 to 1 underdog…
Off-suit over-cards	.40	1.5 to 1
J and an over-card	.31	2.2 to 1
Over-card and an under-card	.48	1.1 to 1
Any two under-cards (not paired or connected)	.69	2.2 to 1 favorite…
Suited connectors below JT, which does not match JT suit	.63	1.7 to 1
Off-suit connectors below JT	.67	2 to 1
A Random Hand	.58	1.4 to 1

76 suited vs.	Probability of Win	Odds
AA	.22	3.5 to 1 underdog...
Over-pair	.21	4 to 1
Any pocket pair below 76	.51	Even
Suited over-cards	.38	1.6 to 1
Off-suit over-cards	.40	1.5 to 1
Over-card and an under-card	.47	1.1 to 1
A Random Hand	.45	1.2 to 1

72 off-suit vs.	Probability of Win	Odds
AA	.12	7 to 1 underdog...
Over-pair	.12	7 to 1
Any pocket pair below 7	.29	2.4 to 1
Suited over-cards	.30	2.3 to 1
Off-suit over-cards	.31	2.2 to 1
Over-card and a card between 2 and 7 (i.e. A6, T5)	.35	1.9 to 1
A Random Hand	.35	1.9 to 1

K6 off-suit vs.	Probability of Win	Odds
AA	.12	7 to 1 underdog...
Under-pair	.46	1.1 to 1
Pair between K and 6	.29	2.4 to 1
AK	.24	3.2 to 1
Ax, where x is between K and 6	.36	1.8 to 1
A5, A4, A3, A2	.40	1.5 to 1
A Random Hand	.54	1.2 to 1 favorite

J8 suited vs.	Probability of Win	Odds
AA	.19	4 to 1 underdog...
Under-pair	.50	Even
Pair between J and 8	.32	2.1 to 1
Over-cards	.37	1.7 to 1
AT and A9	.41	1.4 to 1
Ax, where x is less than 8	.45	1.2 to 1
A Random Hand	.54	1.2 to 1 favorite

Random Hands: Heads-up to a Showdown

‹

Summary

		A	K	Q	J	T	9	8	7	6	5	4	3	2
	OFFSUIT													
S U I T E D	**A**	.85	.67	.66	.65	.65	.63	.62	.61	.60	.60	.59	.58	.57
	K	.65	.82	.63	.63	.62	.60	.58	.58	.57	.56	.55	.54	.53
	Q	.64	.61	.80	.60	.59	.58	.56	.54	.54	.53	.52	.51	.50
	J	.64	.61	.58	.77	.58	.56	.54	.52	.51	.50	.49	.48	.47
	T	.63	.59	.57	.55	.75	.54	.52	.51	.49	.47	.47	.46	.45
	9	.61	.58	.55	.53	.52	.72	.51	.49	.47	.46	.44	.43	.42
	8	.60	.56	.54	.51	.50	.48	.69	.48	.46	.45	.43	.41	.40
	7	.59	.55	.52	.50	.48	.46	.45	.66	.45	.44	.42	.40	.38
	6	.58	.54	.51	.48	.46	.44	.43	.42	.63	.43	.41	.40	.38
	5	.58	.53	.50	.47	.44	.43	.41	.41	.40	.60	.41	.40	.38
	4	.57	.52	.49	.46	.44	.41	.39	.39	.38	.38	.57	.39	.37
	3	.56	.51	.48	.45	.43	.40	.37	.37	.36	.36	.35	.54	.36
	2	.55	.51	.47	.44	.42	.39	.37	.35	.34	.34	.33	.32	.50

*Start with the left hand column for suited hand calculations and the top row for off-suit hand calculations.

higher card 1st.

Pairs vs. a Random Hand	Probability of Win	Odds
AA	.85	6 to 1 favorite…
KK	.82	4.6 to 1
QQ	.80	4 to 1
JJ	.77	3.3 to 1
TT	.75	3 to 1
99	.72	2.6 to 1
88	.69	2.2 to 1
77	.66	1.9 to 1
66	.63	1.7 to 1
55	.60	1.5 to 1
44	.57	1.3 to 1
33	.54	1.2 to 1
22	.50	Even

Ax vs. a Random Hand	Probability of Win	Odds
AA	.85	6 to 1 favorite...
AKs	.67	2 to 1
AK	.65	1.9 to 1
AQs	.66	1.9 to 1
AQ	.64	1.8 to 1
AJs	.65	1.9 to 1
AJ	.64	1.8 to 1
ATs	.65	1.9 to 1
AT	.63	1.7 to 1
A9s	.63	1.7 to 1
A9	.61	1.6 to 1
A8s	.62	1.6 to 1
A8	.60	1.5 to 1
A7s	.61	1.6 to 1
A7	.59	1.4 to 1
A6s	.60	1.5 to 1
A6	.58	1.4 to 1
A5s	.60	1.5 to 1
A5	.58	1.4 to 1
A4s	.59	1.4 to 1
A4	.57	1.3 to 1
A3s	.58	1.4 to 1
A3	.56	1.3 to 1
A2s	.57	1.3 to 1
A2	.55	1.2 to 1

Kx vs. a Random Hand	Probability of Win	Odds
KK	.82	4.6 to 1 favorite…
KQs	.63	1.7 to 1
KQ	.61	1.6 to 1
KJs	.63	1.7 to 1
KJ	.61	1.6 to 1
KTs	.62	1.6 to 1
KT	.60	1.5 to 1
K9s	.60	1.5 to 1
K9	.58	1.4 to 1
K8s	.58	1.4 to 1
K8	.56	1.3 to 1
K7s	.58	1.4 to 1
K7	.55	1.2 to 1
K6s	.57	1.3 to 1
K6	.54	1.2 to 1
K5s	.56	1.3 to 1
K5	.53	1.1 to 1
K4s	.55	1.2 to 1
K4	.52	1.1 to 1
K3s	.54	1.2 to 1
K3	.51	Even
K2s	.53	1.1 to 1
K2	.51	Even

Qx vs. a Random Hand	Probability of Win	Odds
QQ	.80	4 to 1 favorite...
QJs	.60	1.5 to 1
QJ	.58	1.4 to 1
QTs	.59	1.4 to 1
QT	.57	1.3 to 1
Q9s	.58	1.4 to 1
Q9	.55	1.2 to 1
Q8s	.56	1.3 to 1
Q8	.54	1.2 to 1
Q7s	.54	1.2 to 1
Q7	.52	1.1 to 1
Q6s	.54	1.2 to 1
Q6	.51	Even
Q5s	.53	1.1 to 1
Q5	.50	Even
Q4s	.52	1.1 to 1
Q4	.49	Even
Q3s	.51	Even
Q3	.48	1.1 to 1 underdog
Q2s	.50	Even
Q2	.47	1.1 to 1 underdog

Jx vs. a Random Hand	Probability of Win	Odds
JJ	.77	3.3 to 1 favorite…
JTs	.58	1.4 to 1
JT	.55	1.2 to 1
J9s	.56	1.3 to 1
J9	.53	1.1 to 1
J8s	.54	1.2 to 1
J8	.51	Even
J7s	.52	1.1 to 1
J7	.50	Even
J6s	.51	Even
J6	.48	1.1 to 1 underdog
J5s	.50	Even
J5	.47	1.1 to 1 underdog…
J4s	.49	Even
J4	.46	1.2 to 1
J3s	.48	1.1 to 1
J3	.45	1.2 to 1
J2s	.47	1.1 to 1
J2	.44	1.3 to 1

Tx vs. a Random Hand	Probability of Win	Odds
TT	.75	3 to 1 favorite
T9s	.54	1.2 to 1
T9	.52	1.1 to 1
T8s	.52	1.1 to 1
T8	.50	Even
T7s	.51	Even
T7	.48	1.1 to 1 underdog
T6s	.49	Even
T6	.46	1.2 to 1
T5s	.47	1.1 to 1
T5	.44	1.3 to 1
T4s	.47	1.1 to 1
T4	.44	1.3 to 1
T3s	.46	1.2 to 1
T3	.43	1.3 to 1
T2s	.45	1.2 to 1
T2	.42	1.4 to 1

9x vs. a Random Hand	Probability of Win	Odds
99	.72	2.6 to 1 favorite
98s	.51	Even
98	.48	1.1 to 1 underdog
97s	.49	Even
97	.46	1.2 to 1 underdog...
96s	.47	1.1 to 1
96	.44	1.3 to 1
95s	.46	1.2 to 1
95	.43	1.3 to 1
94s	.44	1.3 to 1
94	.41	1.4 to 1
93s	.43	1.3 to 1
93	.40	1.5 to 1
92s	.42	1.4 to 1
92	.39	1.6 to 1

8x vs. a Random Hand	Probability of Win	Odds
88	.69	2.2 to 1 favorite
87s	.48	1.1 to 1 underdog...
87	.45	1.2 to 1
86s	.46	1.2 to 1
86	.43	1.3 to 1
85s	.45	1.2 to 1
85	.41	1.4 to 1
84s	.43	1.3 to 1
84	.39	1.6 to 1
83s	.41	1.4 to 1
83	.37	1.7 to 1
82s	.40	1.5 to 1
82	.37	1.7 to 1

7x vs. a Random Hand	Probability of Win	Odds
77	.66	1.9 to 1 favorite
76s	.45	1.2 to 1 underdog...
76	.42	1.4 to 1
75s	.44	1.3 to 1
75	.41	1.4 to 1
74s	.42	1.4 to 1
74	.39	1.6 to 1
73s	.40	1.5 to 1
73	.37	1.7 to 1
72s	.38	1.6 to 1
72	.35	1.9 to 1

6x vs. a Random Hand	Probability of Win	Odds
66	.63	1.7 to 1 favorite
65s	.43	1.3 to 1 underdog…
65	.40	1.5 to 1
64s	.41	1.4 to 1
64	.38	1.6 to 1
63s	.40	1.5 to 1
63	.36	1.8 to 1
62s	.38	1.6 to 1
62	.34	1.9 to 1

5x vs. a Random Hand	Probability of Win	Odds
55	.60	1.5 to 1 favorite
54s	.41	1.4 to 1 underdog...
54	.38	1.6 to 1
53s	.40	1.5 to 1
53	.36	1.8 to 1
52s	.38	1.6 to 1
52	.34	1.9 to 1

4x vs. a Random Hand	Probability of Win	Odds
44	.57	1.3 to 1 favorite
43s	.39	1.6 to 1 underdog...
43	.35	1.9 to 1
42s	.37	1.7 to 1
42	.33	2 to 1

3x vs. a Random Hand	Probability of Win	Odds
33	.54	1.2 to 1 favorite
32s	.36	1.8 to 1 underdog...
32	.32	2.1 to 1

Appendix

Starting Hand Guidelines from
Internet Texas Hold'em

The starting hand guidelines in these charts are taken from Matthew's first book, *Internet Texas Hold'em*. The charts are intended as a guideline for beginning to intermediate players playing in typical Limit games on the Internet.

Early Position	Unraised Pot	Raised Pot
AA KK QQ	Raise	Reraise
JJ	Call	Call
TT 99	Call	Fold
88 77	Call 1	Fold
AKs AK	Raise	Reraise
AQs AQ AJs	Raise	Call
AJ ATs A9s	Call	Fold
A8s A7s	Call 1	Fold
KQs	Call	Fold
KJs	Call 1	Fold
QJs	Call 1	Fold

Middle Position	Unraised Pot	Raised Pot
AA KK QQ	Raise	Reraise
JJ	Raise First in, Call 1	Call
TT	Raise First in, Call 1	Fold
99	Call	Fold
88 77	Call 1	Fold
66 55	Call 2	Fold
44 33 22	Call 3	Fold
AKs AK	Raise	Reraise
AQs AQ AJs	Raise	Call
AJ ATs AT	Raise First in, Call 1	Fold
A9s A8s A7s	Call	Fold
Axs	Call 1	Fold
KQs KQ KJs	Call	Fold
KTs	Call 1	Fold
QJs QTs	Call 1	Fold
JTs	Call 2	Fold
J9s	Call 3	Fold
T9s	Call 3	Fold
98s	Call 3	Fold

Late Position	Unraised Pot	Raised Pot
AA KK QQ	Raise	Reraise (RR)
JJ TT	Raise 1, Call 2	RR 1 Option, Call All
99	Raise First In, Call 1	RR or Fold against 1 player, Call 3
88 77	Raise First In, Call 1	Call 3
66 55	Call 2	Call 4
44 33 22	Call 3	Call 4
AKs AK	Raise	Reraise
AQs AQ AJs	Raise	RR 1 option, Call All
AJ ATs	Raise 1, Call 2	Fold
AT Axs	Raise First In, Call 1	Fold
A9	Raise First In; otherwise Fold	Fold
KQs	Raise 1, Call 2	Call
KQ KJs KJ KTs	Raise First In, Call 1	Fold
KT K9s	Call 2	Fold
K8s K7s	Call 3	Fold
Kxs	Call 4	Fold
QJs	Raise First In, Call 1	Call 4
QJ QTs	Raise First In, Call 1	Fold
QT Q9s	Call 2	Fold
Q8s	Call 4	Fold
JTs	Raise First In, Call 1	Call 4
JT	Call 3	Fold
J9s	Call 2	Fold
J8s	Call 4	Fold
T9s	Call 2	Call 5
T8s	Call 3	Fold
98s	Call 3	Call 5
87s	Call 4	Fold
76s	Call 4	Fold

BLINDS	SB Unraised Pot	SB Raised Pot	BB Raised Pot*
AA KK QQ	Raise	Reraise (RR)	Reraise (raise limpers)
JJ	Raise 1, Call 2	RR 1, Call 2	Call (raise 1 limper)
TT 99	Raise 1, Call 2	RR 1, Call 2	Call
88 77	Call	RR Lone Late, Call 3	Call 2, or 1 Middle or Late
66 55	Call	Call 3	Call 2, or 1 Late
44 33 22	Call	Call 3	Call 2
AKs	Raise	Reraise (RR)	Reraise (raise limpers)
AK	Raise	Reraise or Call	Reraise or Call (raise limpers)
AQs AQ	Raise 1 or 2, Call 3	RR 1 or 2, Call 3	Call (raise 1 or 2 limpers)
AJs ATs	Raise 1, Call 2	RR Lone Late, Call 1	Call
AJ AT	Raise 1, Call 2	RR Lone Late, Fold	Call
A9s	Call	RR Lone Late, Fold	Call
A9 A8	Call	Fold	Call 1 Late, Fold
Axs Ax	Call	Fold	Axs Call, Ax Fold
KQs	Call	Call 2, or 1 Late	Call
KQ	Call	Fold	Call
KJs	Call	Call 4, or 1 Late	Call
KJ	Call	Fold	Call 2, or 1 Late
KTs	Call	Fold	Call
KT	Call	Fold	Call 2, or 1 Late
K9s	Call	Fold	Call
Kxs	Call	Fold	Call 3
QJs	Call	Call 4	Call
QJ QTs QT	Call	Fold	Call
Q9s Q8s	Call	Fold	Call 2, or 1 Late
Qxs	Call 3	Fold	Call 3
JTs	Call	Call 4	Call
JT J9s	Call	Fold	Call 2
J8s	Call	Fold	Call 3
J7s	Call 3	Fold	Call 5
T9s	Call	Call 5	Call 2
T9 T8s	Call	Fold	Call 3
T7s	Call 3	Fold	Call 4
98s	Call	Call 5	Call 2
98 97s	Call 2	Fold	Call 3
96s	Call 4	Fold	Call 5
87s	Call	Fold	Call 3
87 86s	Call 3	Fold	Call 4
85s	Call 4	Fold	Fold
76s	Call	Fold	Call 3
76 75s	Call 3	Fold	Call 4
65s	Call 2	Fold	Call 3
65 64s	Call 3	Fold	Fold
54s	Call 2	Fold	Call 4
54 53s 43s 32s	Call 4	Fold	Fold

* In the Big Blind, cap with AA, KK, and sometimes QQ. Only call reraises with JJ, AKs, AK, AQs, AQ, and AJs. Raise limpers where indicated

Glossary

Action: Frequency of betting. A game or hand with a lot of action is one where there is a lot of betting and raising.

Acting First: The player who must check or bet before the other players *is acting first.*

Acting Last: The last player to check, bet, call, or raise is *acting last.*

All-in: A player who bets the last amount of chips he has or is disconnected while playing a hand.

Backdoor: A draw that requires both the turn *and* river card to improve. For example, the turn and river card are both suited, giving you a backdoor-flush. Same as runner-runner.

Bad Beat: A hand that loses to an opponent who gets very lucky, especially when the opponent should not even have played his hand.

Bankroll: The money you have available to gamble.

Bet: The action of being the first player to commit chips to the pot on any given betting round.

Bettor: The first person to commit chips to the pot on any given betting round.

Big Bet: The amount of the bet on the last two rounds of betting.

Blinds: In Hold'em, the blinds are the forced bets that the first two players to the left of the button must put in the pot. The big blind posts a small bet and the small blind usually posts a half small bet.

Bluff: A bet or raise when you have little chance of winning the pot if you are called.

Board: The community cards on the table.

Bottom Pair: A pair made by matching one of your hole cards with the lowest card on the board or a pocket pair lower than all of the cards on the board.

Button: Also known as the dealer. The last player to receive cards and, subsequently, the last player to act on the flop, turn, and river. The blinds sit to the immediate left of the button.

Call: To put money in the pot equal to an opponent's bet or raise.

Call a Raise Cold: To call a raise without having committed money previously on the same betting round. Note how this is different than betting or calling and then calling a raise by another opponent.

Caller: A player who puts money in the pot equal to the bet or raise.

Cap: The act of putting in the last raise allowable on any given betting round. A capped pot is one where the maximum number of raises has been reached.

Check: Declining to bet.

Check-raise: The act of checking and then raising after an opponent bets.

Close the Betting: Making the last call on any given betting round.

Cold Call: see Call a Raise Cold.

Crying Call: Calling when you feel you have a very small chance of winning.

Cutoff: The player who acts right before the button or dealer.

Dead Money: Money put into the pot by players who have already folded. The blinds and antes are dead money once those players have folded.

Dealer: The dealer position is the same as the button position.

Discount: Reducing the odds for drawing to an out by the probability that the out is no good or you are drawing dead.

Disregard: You should disregard an out when you are drawing dead to it.

Double Belly-buster: A hand with two gut-shot draws. For example, you hold JT and the flop comes AQ8.

Douts: Discounted outs.

Drawing Dead: Drawing with no chance of improving to the winning hand.

Early position: In a ten-handed game, the first three seats to the left of the blinds. After the flop, early position refers to players who must act first.

Effective Implied Pot Odds: The relationship between the current pot and the best you expect to win compared to the current bet.

Expectation: The average result on any play in the long run.

Favorite: The hand that has the best chance of winning. Note that sometimes you could be the favorite without currently having the best-made hand. For example, an open-ended straight flush draw is the favorite over a pair.

First-In: The first player who commits chips to the pot.

Fish: A poor player who usually loses money. Generally refers to players who draw to very weak hands and often play many poor starting hands.

Flop: The betting round where three cards have been dealt face up.

Fold: Giving up on a hand rather than calling a bet or raise.

Folding Equity: Refers to when you have enough chips in your stack to put pressure on your opponents to fold. A big concern with a small stack is that you do not have folding equity to steal the blinds and will be forced to a showdown.

Free Card: A card that you can see without having to call a bet.

Full Table: A game with nine or ten players.

Gut-shot: A draw to a straight where only one card can give you the straight.

Heads-up: A pot contested against a lone opponent.

Implied Pot Odds: The relationship between the current pot and the potential bets you could win compared to the current bet.

Induce a Bluff: Playing your hand weakly so that an opponent might try a bluff.

Induce a Call: Playing your hand weakly so that an opponent might make a crying call.

Kicker: The other card in your hand that has not matched the board.

Late Position: In a ten-handed game, the last two seats at the table generally known as the cutoff position in seat nine and the button in seat ten.

Limp: The act of calling first-in before the flop.

Lone Opponent: When only one opponent is contesting the pot.

Loose: A player who plays many hands. After the flop, a loose player will often play to the river and will frequently try to bluff. A game is loose when there are a lot of players who see the flop.

Maniac: A super aggressive player who is constantly raising the pot and plays most of his hands.

Middle/Bottom Pair: A pair below the highest card on the table.

Middle Position: In a ten-handed game, seats six, seven, and eight.

Nuts: Holding the best possible hand on any given betting round.

Odds: The chance against an event happening.

Open: The first player to commit chips to the pot other than the blind money.

Open-ended Straight: A straight that can be made by two different cards.

Outs: A card that will improve your hand, preferably to the winning hand.

Over-card: A card higher than the highest card on the board.

Over-pair: A pocket pair higher than the highest card on the board.

Pocket Pair: Holding a pair with the two cards dealt to you.

Position: The order in which you have to act. You are in early position if acting first and late position if acting last.

Pot-committed: When the ratio of the pot versus the amount of chips you have left is so high that calling with any hand is profitable.

Pot Odds: The relationship between the total amount in the pot to the amount of the current bet.

Pre-flop: The first betting round when the players receive their two hole cards.

Probability: The chance that an event will occur, often expressed in percentage terms.

Protect: Betting or raising so that your opponents must pay a price to try and draw to beat you.

Rag: A board card lower than a 9.

Rainbow: A flop with three different suits.

Raise: To increase the bet an additional amount.

Read: Determining the possible hands of your opponent.

Re-buy: The act of purchasing additional chips.

Re-raise: To increase an opponent's raise an additional amount.

Ring Game: A full table cash game with nine to ten players.

River: The fifth board card.

Rock: A player who is very tight and rarely bluffs.

Runner-runner: A draw that requires both the turn *and* river card to improve. For example, the turn and river card are both suited giving you a backdoor-flush.

Scare Card: A card that is potentially dangerous to either you or your opponent.

Semi-bluff: A bet or raise, in which if called, you probably do not have the best hand, but you could improve to the best hand on the next card.

Set: Three of a kind when holding a pocket pair that matches one of the board cards.

Shark: A very good player.

Short-handed: Refers to games when only several players are playing. Some sites specifically offer short-handed games that only allow up to 5 or 6 players at the table.

Short-stacked: A player who does not have very many chips left to bet.

Slow-play: Checking or just calling a very strong hand on one round of betting to win more bets on later rounds of betting.

Small Bet: The amount of the bet on the first two rounds of betting.

Split the Pot: Dividing the pot equally between two or more opponents who showdown the same hand.

Steal: Raising to win the blinds pre-flop. Stealing the pot on later betting rounds is the same as a bluff.

Street: A betting round such as the flop, turn, or river.

Stretch: Refers to straight draws that cannot be completed in one direction by an ace limiting how far the straight can go. For example, AK can only make a straight in one direction with QJT. AK does not stretch since a straight with this hand cannot include a 2.

Strong: Term to describe good poker players.

Table Image: Refers to how a player is perceived to play. Generally relates to how tight or loose a player is.

Tell: An act or gesture that *might* indicate how strong or weak your opponent's hand might be.

Tight: A player who does not play very many hands. After the flop, tight players rarely bluff and generally only continue to play with strong hands or strong draws. A game is tight when there are not very many players who see the flop.

Tilt: A player who starts playing recklessly and wild because he is upset and angry.

Top Pair: A pair using one of your hole cards to match the highest card on the board.

Trap Hands: Hands that typically are dominated by other hands, such as KJ, KT, and QT. These hands rarely win large pots, unless you hit a straight, and can lose a lot of money to hands with better kickers or players with good draws.

Trips: Three of a kind when one of your pocket cards matches a pair on the board.

Turn: The fourth board card.

Under the Gun: The first player to act pre-flop in early position.

Weak: Term to describe poor poker players. They generally play too many hands pre-flop and will often call too often after the flop.